The ULTIMATE Chiropractic Start-Up Guide

How to start a practice from nothing and become a chiro super success!

For more information:

Tory M. Robson DC
7114 Shady Oak Road
Eden Prairie, MN 55344

Dedication

To all the men and women since 1895 who have
had the courage and vision to go out on their own and
dedicate their professional lives to serving humanity with
this incredible phenomenon called Chiropractic.

These are my uncensored thoughts and
unapologetic opinions gained from the real and
often unforgiving world of chiropractic practice
and consulting. For legal or financial questions
always consult the appropriate accountants,
attorneys, and professional advisors.

TABLE OF CONTENTS

Simplicity is the ultimate form of sophistication.
-*Bruce Lee*

When it comes to starting, growing, and succeeding in practice why would you listen to Dr. Tory Robson of **PRO**SPINE Health and Injury Center and **WINNERS**EDGE Chiropractic Consulting?

Why would you now find yourself reading carefully, wanting to learn more, and doing what I recommend to succeed?

Consider-

- I have done <u>exactly</u> what you want to do, and that is build a super successful chiropractic office. I've done it many times now. I built my first office from a dirt floor and was profitable within 30 days.

- Outgrowing this office, I then designed and built my second office from a bare floor. With just one great CA we grew this office to 130 patients a day in record time.

- I wanted to live in a bigger city so I sold this practice and moved to Minneapolis. Starting with an empty space, I designed and built my third office. Using all my methods, I attracted 259 new patients in my first 90 days open and was well over 300 patients a week practically overnight.

- A few years later I bought several units in a Class A office development in my area. I built an amazing new office and moved my practice there. I now owned my office space and was a commercial landlord to a few other tenants. Having been a commercial real estate landlord is incredibly valuable. Rent is one of the most expensive elements in practice. My experience here has saved my clients tens of thousands on their leases.

- My practice success and ability to design, start, and grow practices prompted many to ask if I might do some coaching. Seeing the future, I sold this practice to a new doctor. As far as we know this was the highest selling single doctor office ever in Minnesota. I then rented a space in a western suburb of Minneapolis. Here I would be closer to the airport and the chiropractic college.

- Now in Eden Prairie, I designed and built a beautiful and efficient 1150 ft. office also from a grey shell. In under a year I was collecting $70,000 a month practicing just 12-16 hours a week.

Listen carefully-

- After 5 great years at this location the rent was set to go up to $4000 a month. I thought: *$4000 per month for 1150 ft. Hmm... there's got to be a better way.* I then asked myself this question: *How can I have a perfect new office and pay less rent?*

- After some hard thinking I figured out how to do it and started building my sixth brand new office in an 11,200 ft. Martial Arts and Fitness Center. Not only is this my sweet new office, but it also serves as the WINNER**SEDGE** Chiro Training Center.

Now follow this-

- I engineered a deal where I pay <u>no rent</u> for 10 years. This saves me over $480,000 in rent. In addition, I was able to create a situation where I actually get paid $6000 every month.

- I have an amazing practice and consulting office with the best location in the city plus it's inside a fitness center. I created an environment where everybody wins and I get paid to be here.

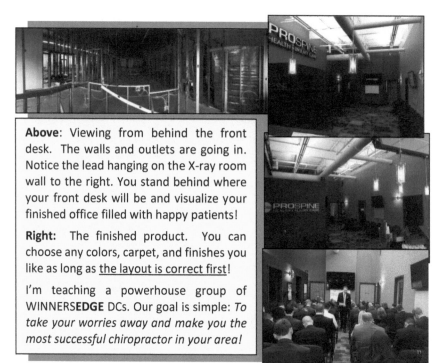

Above: Viewing from behind the front desk. The walls and outlets are going in. Notice the lead hanging on the X-ray room wall to the right. You stand behind where your front desk will be and visualize your finished office filled with happy patients!

Right: The finished product. You can choose any colors, carpet, and finishes you like as long as <u>the layout is correct first</u>!

I'm teaching a powerhouse group of WINNER**SEDGE** DCs. Our goal is simple: *To take your worries away and make you the most successful chiropractor in your area!*

Most chiropractors will pay around $360,000 over 10 years for their office rent. I, on the other hand, <u>will get paid $480,000</u>. This places me ahead of the typical doctor by $840,000 in just 10 years. My ability to create successful solutions from nothing is why so many call me.

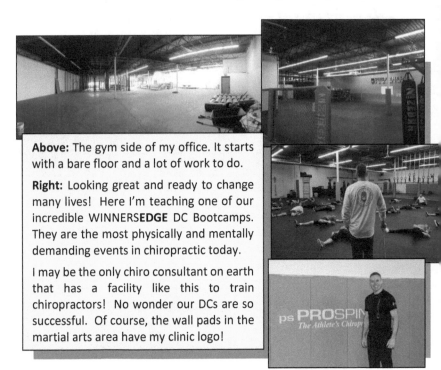

Above: The gym side of my office. It starts with a bare floor and a lot of work to do.

Right: Looking great and ready to change many lives! Here I'm teaching one of our incredible WINNER**S**EDGE DC Bootcamps. They are the most physically and mentally demanding events in chiropractic today.

I may be the only chiro consultant on earth that has a facility like this to train chiropractors! No wonder our DCs are so successful. Of course, the wall pads in the martial arts area have my clinic logo!

- I've now published three books, 33 Audio and DVD sets, plus over 1000 videos on all elements of practice start-up and success.

- I have taught over 100 Seminars, Bootcamps, and Trainings to DCs and Teams at all levels of practice.

- I have had over 50,000 coaching calls with chiropractors giving me literally hundreds of years of experience to share.

- I stopped counting after having designed and advised the building of over 100 new practices. At any given time I have 5 to 25 practices around the country either being built or remodeled using my designs and specifications.

I can talk until I'm blue in the face but nothing will matter until YOU have the practice YOU want so YOU can create a great life!

The average chiropractor today sees around 90 patients a week and collects $20,000 per month. Your goal is to never be average.

Read these carefully and picture yourself as one of them. Call and talk to them! This is our first step in positioning your mind for success.

Dr. Ryan Alter - *Delray Beach, FL*

I have a sweet new office, I have broken every practice record many times, and I have a beautiful new house with an amazing pool. Using his money systems, I save and have paid all practice and student loans making a $500,000+ change in my net worth. I've been with Tory for 9 years, he's incredible.

Drs. Kerri Norring and Karrie Lehn - *Andover, MN*

We opened our new Tory designed office and with our split schedule we hit 386 visits a week within two weeks. His systems, money, and CA training have changed our lives. We absolutely LOVE it! Our families also love how much we have grown!

Dr. Rich Sheppard - *Hickory, NC*

I was average when I joined with Tory. I did what he said and now my 3 CAs and I just saw 164 visits in one day and had our best collection month ever at $101,517. Tory is awesome. Hearing my kids laugh as they jump in our new pool is absolutely priceless!

Dr. Joe Parpala - *Hermantown, MN*

*I joined Tory's **Mach1** program before I started in practice. 200 patients in one day is now normal for me. I love my office! Me and my two CAs had 66 new patients last month and I do NO marketing. Plus, my family and I love our new house on the lake!*

Drs. Jay Lang, Mike Zauhar & Mike O'Day - *Brainerd, MN*

Tory was my roommate in chiro school. We collected $272,000 <u>more</u> our first year in his Mach1 program. He took my practice worries away. Now we are all ready to break our records again!

Dr. Greg Oleson - *Armstrong, IA*

I was not happy in practice so I joined with Tory. I did exactly what he taught me. Now I have a 400 visit a week office plus me and my CA team just hit a new best collections of over $140,000 in one month. My fitness, savings, and fun levels are also through the roof! My life has completely changed with WINNERSEDGE.

Dr. Jonathan Olson - *Minneapolis, MN*

I was flatlined for several years then joined with Tory. Now after breaking all our practice records my associate Dr. Matt and I are wrapping up another record year of over $1.2M. I'm so glad I'm in WINNERSEDGE, Tory is the real deal!

Dr. Art Hoffman - *Hopkins, MN*

Tory designed my office, I have done the Bootcamps, I use his goal setting and practice systems, I am a GUARDIAN member within the WINNERSEDGE group and I just had my first month of collecting over $100,000. Yes, just me and my two great CAs!

Dr. Beth Eyles - *Deerfield, IL*

I joined with Tory and grew to $50,000+ per month and my money flow has been totally overhauled! Plus me and my CA love the Seminars and the Bootcamps, they are awesome!

Dr. Nate Deines - *Sheridan, WY*

In my new Tory designed office we're at 400 patient visits a week plus me and my 3 CAs just collected $105,000 in a month. My family and I just moved into our dream home and we totally love it. Tory is the man. Plain and simple.

Dr. Kevin Wilmot - *Kalispell, MT*

Tory was my first chiropractor in 1996! He inspired me then and now a DC myself I have a best of 172 visits in one <u>afternoon</u>. My family and I love the view of Whitefish Lake and Big Mountain ski area from the deck of our new home! Tory is the best. If you want to win in practice and in life join us here at WINNERSEDGE!

in-ten-tion *noun* 1. a thing intended, an aim or plan.

vi-sion *noun* 1. the ability to think or plan the future with imagination or wisdom.
2. a mental image of what the future will or could be like.

When opening a practice, we must already know what it should look like in its complete and perfected state. An architect's drawing has every detail and usage need of a space considered before anything is ever built. We must do the same.

The most successful people always have an image in their mind of perfection with whatever they are doing. It may be a golf shot, an artist doing a painting, a chiropractor giving an adjustment, or you building a new office and then building your practice within it.

General Guide on Capacity:

- **1 DC no CA:** With incredible systems and an office under 600 ft., one DC doing pure chiropractic and no therapy can get to 50 a day or 200 visits a week. It is a fair amount of work but it can be done. It can cause a doctor to wear down so systems are critical. Hiring a CA at the right time is recommended.

- **1 DC and 1 CA:** In a pure chiropractic office with no therapy and incredibly efficient systems a DC can get to 100 patients a day. In an office that uses any therapy that requires CA time, then 50 patients a day is more realistic.

- **1 DC and 2 CAs:** This is the sweet spot where a doctor can help as many patients as they can handle with or without therapy.

- **1 DC and 3 CAs:** Can handle anything one DC can generate.

- **2 DCs and no CA:** Working together can get to 50 patients a day.

- **2 DCs and 1 CA:** All 3 working together, maybe 75 in a day if purely adjusting with no therapy.

- **2 DCs and 2 CAs:** Can reach 100 visits a day.

- **2 DCs and 3 CAs:** Can reach 150 a day.

- **2 DCs and 4 CAs:** Can reach 200 a day.

Two doctors in one office means you must double <u>everything</u> to have any chance of getting 100% output from each doctor. It has been proven for years that two doctors in one office normally amounts to about 1.2 doctor's worth of production every month.

Have you ever tied one leg to a friend's leg and ran a three-legged race? Did you run faster or slower? A clinic owner may "think" they have extra time and space for another doctor but this is an illusion.

If you add another doctor you need to double the parking spots, double the chairs, double the computers, double the number of X-ray machines, double the staff, double the bathrooms, double the equipment, double the phone lines, double the credit card machines, double the square footage, double everything if you want each doctor to produce 100%.

Observe the image below. Imagine the dots are people in your office. Notice that for every person you add how many more lines, friction points, and management needs that are created. More than one doctor in a chiropractic office requires incredibly capable coaching to have any chance of success. Call me immediately if you are considering this.

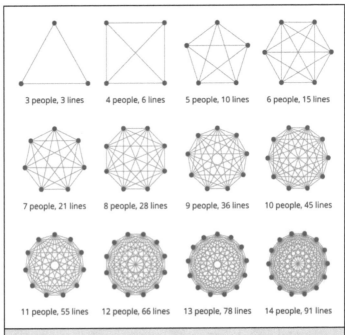

3 people, 3 lines	4 people, 6 lines	5 people, 10 lines	6 people, 15 lines
7 people, 21 lines	8 people, 28 lines	9 people, 36 lines	10 people, 45 lines
11 people, 55 lines	12 people, 66 lines	13 people, 78 lines	14 people, 91 lines

See why 1 DC with 2 CAs is the sweet spot for high production with low overhead? I can coach anything, but I do want you to be aware of what happens when you add people to a business.

The doctor above did not want to listen to me. They instead wanted to tell me how great they were even though they were making no money and couldn't sleep at night. People often want to defend what is <u>not</u> working. Please remember this: *We never defend what is not working!*

This is an extremely complex situation with countless ramifications and legal exposure at every turn. In a nutshell, my coaching plan was to sell one office immediately, then get the remaining office running well with the DC owner plus the best associate doctor and 2 best staff.

This doctor finally listened to me and made the smart moves with my guidance. This doctor now sleeps like a baby with their highly profitable, low stress, and fun practice.

Now back to YOUR intention and vision.

Questions:

- How many people do you really want to see per week?
- How much will this volume collect per month?
- How many staff will you need?
- Where will each employee be able to sit and work in the office?
- In perfected form, what does your office look like on a busy day?

- How much interest will be due each month on your student loans?
- How much will you be paying on them a year after opening?
- When will you have your student loans paid in full?
- When do you plan to buy a house?
- Are you married or planning on it? If so, when and at what cost?
- Do you have or want kids? How will this affect your practice?

At one of our intense **WINNERSEDGE DC BOOTCAMPS** we had our first billionaire *Zoom call* in and speak to us. This person was so impressive I could write 100 pages on it. He said that ALL top companies <u>and</u> top people know WHY they do what they do. Same is true for us!

One interesting thing is that he never talked about doing anything for money. His efforts were all about being great, creating great, and delivering great things to millions of people. Money is simply a by-product. Money naturally follows when we do valuable things for a massive amount of people.

- **WHY** are you opening a practice?
- **WHY** will you go to work each day?
- **WHY** do you wake up each day?
- **WHY** are you on this planet?

All these require an answer. I can't answer these for you. The most successful doctors know WHY they are here.

We open a practice so we can have a command center to change as many lives as possible with natural chiropractic care. We go to work each day to pursue this MISSION!

We wake up to become better so we can <u>reach more people in a positive way</u>.

We are on this planet so we can leave it, and all those we interacted with, better than when we found them.

The WINNERSEDGE Orange Card. This card has your Definite Chief Aim plus goals for Love, Health, Career and Money. No wonder we are incredibly successful. All WE DCs carry their goals in their wallet at all times.

The above visualization drill is a secret tool of the ultra-succeeder. Once you sign a lease and have secured a space for your new office, you can sit in the parking lot and visualize. When inside the space you can stand where each room will be and picture what will happen in each room.

Take it from me, this works so well it is amazing. Will you actually do this? Or will you make the costly mental error of thinking you are too smart to follow the non-negotiable and unwavering natural laws of success? Everything you want must be in your mind <u>first</u>.

Know Your Story:

I ask students all the time: *What are you going to do when you graduate?* They say: *I don't know* or: *I think I want to be an associate for a while.* Some say: *I might go back home to practice* or: *I'm thinking about starting a practice in Arizona.*

None of these are wrong, but notice how vague, lazy, and un-inspiring they all are. There is a <u>much better way</u>. You must get YOUR STORY down clear and concise!

Once again, this requires <u>thinking</u>. Let me clarify, going to school is not thinking. Talking to friends is not thinking. Being awake and going through the day requires almost no thinking. Most people over the course of a year only really <u>think hard</u> a few times. Once confronted with a problem, people mentally quit and want someone else to just give them an answer. Be a person who is not afraid to use their brain and think.

To give you an idea:

> Draw a floorplan for your perfect office on a blank piece of graph paper. Make sure all the room sizes are correct for all equipment to fit. Have all outlets in the right place to handle all computers, the credit card machine, a fax machine, and all printers.

> Plan the lighting and location of all light switches so kids coming in won't play with them. Select four paint colors and mark exactly what color goes on each wall. Choose the door size, finish color, and the color for the door trim. Make sure all the door swings are correct so the doors won't hit anything when they open.

> Consider what type of locksets, flooring, base trim, along with where the heat and AC vents are to be located to counteract the air coming in the front door. Design the details of your front desk.

A builder will be waiting for all this information and 100 more things <u>before</u> they can build anything.

It has been said for decades and I agree: *There is no activity in the world that people will avoid more than that of sustained thinking.*

Don't be average. Seek to be in the 5% who can figure things out! You will grow to the level of <u>your ability to think</u> and solve problems.

Now back to your story. You want to articulate it smartly using a timeline and real numbers. A goal is not a goal until it has a date attached.

Story example:

> *I graduate November 18th and will have my state license in December. I plan to have my new office open by February 1st.*

> *By May 1st I expect to be seeing at least 100 patients a week and growing from there to over 50 patients per day.*

> *I will implement the WINNERSEDGE office systems and money flow strategy so I can continue to grow and have my student loans completely paid within 5 years. I am so excited to get going!*

Your story is the first statement that indicates your mind is clear and that you have a plan. This clarity, along with your vision and intention, makes you unstoppable. Your life goes to where your mind already is.

In a nutshell our goal is:

- To help as many people as possible
- In as small a space as possible
- With the fewest staff possible
- Collecting as much as possible
- With the lowest overhead possible
- While saving as much as possible
- Getting our debt as low as possible
- Being in the best shape possible
- With as happy a home life as possible

We want it ALL! This is what we teach here at WINNERSEDGE. If this is what you are looking for, you are in the right place.

Every chiropractor has a story, several stories actually. Most just don't know what they are. You must be able to tell a story of why you became a chiropractor, why someone should choose you as their chiropractor, and what your plans and goals are.

If you are a student, complete the following and memorize it. You will be amazed at how soon you will have an opportunity to say it.

So, what are your plans after graduation?

Well, I graduate on _____ and I should have my state license by _____ then I plan to start in my new practice on _____ and then with my coaching, systems, and promotion be seeing over 100 patients every week on or before _____ then grow to over 50 patients per day from there. I plan to have all my money flow systems in place by _____ and should have my student loans paid off by _____. I'm pumped to get rolling and change some lives!

Prepare to Work:

Your thoughts are right. You can see your practice in action and you have the best intentions. Now - Do you realize the amount of work required to be successful? Most people have a job. They go to work, somebody else or some company tells them what to do, then they go home.

These people say things like: *Thank God it's Friday* and: *I hate Mondays* and: *I can't wait for my vacation* and other statements that reveal they are not doing anything they are passionate about.

You may be programmed to think like this and not even know it. Realize there are basically two types of working people in the world. Those few that <u>own</u> a business and those who work for somebody who does.

Those that don't own a business will never understand what it is like to own one. You, however, already know what it's like to have a job.

My truck is the only car there. This is what success looks like. Going in to be productive when nobody else is willing to. I say to clients: *Tell your family and friends you will see them later, you must be dedicated to your business now if you want it to succeed!*

Family and friends will often not understand why you are working the hours you work. They may never understand why you do the things you do or attend the events you do. Many just have a job and are unaware of the demands of owning and operating a successful business.

Learn right now to be strong, but nice, when comments come up like *Why do you have to go in on a Saturday morning?* or *Why can't you get home sooner* or *Why do you have to keep going to those seminars, don't you know everything yet?*

It is critical to know how to work hard. Take pride in your ability to work. *Nobody works harder than me* is what I say. In fact, I recommend all new doctors spend one Friday morning from 4am to Saturday at 6pm in their office. Yes, 38 hours straight in the office working. Sleep on a chiropractic table, bring food but do not leave until 6pm Saturday night. This will make a regular workday ridiculously easy!

We Are On a MISSION:

We own a business and have a MISSION. The mission is to reach as many people as possible and change their lives with incredible chiropractic care. Considering thousands of people around you right now are suffering and you can help them, it is no time to be lazy.

Chiropractic and running an efficient business are lifelong pursuits. This means we must be willing to work harder and working hard never feels like work when you are on a mission!

I am typing this paragraph at 4:58am on a Sunday morning. I am ON a MISSION and being ON a MISSION never feels like work.

You be the Coach:

A doctor has the following stats:

- The chiropractor is under one year in practice.
- He is only seeing 80 visits per week.
- He is not yet paying the full amount due on his student loans.
- The DC is not paying down any debt.
- The DC is not saving any money each month.
- The DC has a negative net worth of around -$325,000.

This DC calls you and asks: *Hey coach, can I take Fridays off yet?*

What is your answer Coach?

The answer is: Are you kidding me? A four-day work week must be earned first. This doctor has yet to learn how to work! Their current mindset has them on the road to struggling painfully for years.

This doctor says he wants to spend more time with his family. This sounds noble, but what **he needs to do** is make more money. Popular saying: *If you love your family, you will work hard to make sure they are financially well taken care of!*

He needs to be in the practice 10 shifts every week plus one hour every Saturday morning until the office is collecting enough to engage the entire WINNERSEDGE money flow system. Then and only then can he take Friday afternoons off.

Once well established, collecting a surplus, and debt is reducing can this doctor even consider another minute off. A refined schedule is the reward for hard and smart work. We have doctors working just at 16 hours a week now. They earned it first and so can you!

Talking about vision, intention, and the mindset required to start a practice can be very nebulous. Visualizing a practice is not that easy to do. What is a practice anyway? The office or clinic includes the space, equipment, employees, and all the material elements. The practice on the other hand, is all the patients, momentum, production, goodwill, and reputation you have created in and outside the office.

We make sure all the office elements are coming together. Then, to get more clarity as far as the actual practice is concerned, we define it with numbers. We can actually CREATE a practice with numbers. To do this we create GOALS and keep STATS.

Earl Nightingale, the father of personal development said: *A successful person is a person who has written down goals.* He is so right!

A practice can be defined by visits per week, collections, new patients, referrals, and several other metrics. It is easy to determine the health of a practice, all you need is to look at the doctor's stats.

We have a very specific way we create our practice goals. We even have several videos and a printed guide on how to do this properly. Our doctors are very successful because they have clear goals and keep stats.

Along with written down goals and keeping stats you must always know what your "Bests" are. Your primary BESTS are your best visits in a day, a week, and your best collections for a day, a week, and a month.

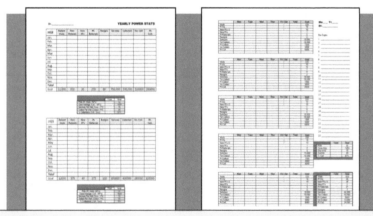

Left: Our Yearly Goal and Stat sheet for two years. **Right**: Our Monthly sheet. Being able to read these is not important yet. What is important is knowing that you want one sheet for each month and a yearly sheet to track the monthly numbers. Don't be fooled, these two sheets of paper are worth millions of dollars to those who use them.

There Is No Such Thing as Competition:

A final point regarding vision and intention is a discussion about the difference between COMPETITION and CREATION in practice.

A common low-level comment is: *Gee there are a lot of chiropractors around.* This type of language comes from a mind that thinks they are "competing" with others. They think there are a limited number of new patients and that we must all "compete" for them.

I don't have enough time to explain how wrong this type of thinking is. The fact is: <u>We all CREATE our own practice</u>. There is not one pie, we all create our own pie. You will create your own practice. There are unlimited people out there. Yes, unlimited!

I have a client in a town of 900 people. He has had over 8000 new patients in the last 20 years. How is this possible? It is possible because people don't live in a city - they flow through a city. <u>There are unlimited people.</u> The only competition you have is between you and yourself!

The more chiropractors in an area the better! This means there is more chiropractic awareness and a lot more people going to the chiropractor! Every chiropractor wins!

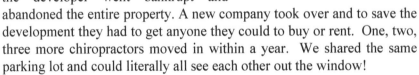

In the picture you see me having fun in front of an office building I owned. I bought into this office complex with the agreement that I would be the only chiropractor allowed in any of the ten buildings in this development.

The real estate crisis hit in 2008, the developer went bankrupt and abandoned the entire property. A new company took over and to save the development they had to get anyone they could to buy or rent. One, two, three more chiropractors moved in within a year. We shared the same parking lot and could literally all see each other out the window!

The small, fearful, competitive type thinker would have been furious and complained like a crybaby. But what did I do? <u>I rented extra space in my office to a 4th chiropractor</u>! I then went on to break all my clinic collection records one after another. There is no such thing as competition in chiropractic. Winners CREATE their own circumstances. Winners create their own luck. Winners always figure out a way to win!

Getting Specific With Goals:

When we start coaching a chiropractor who wants to open a successful office we immediately set clear goals. Many doctors will never do this properly their entire career. This is one of many reasons why so few chiropractors in the world ever become ultra-successful.

Having smart and accurate goals can take a struggling doctor and get them above water. Smart goals can take an average doctor and make them above average. If a doctor is already an achiever, the right goal and stat system like we teach will propel them to super success!

The new doctor will not know what goals to set, what numbers to use, and have no reference point for what is good, bad, right, or wrong.

The main goals we set are for the year we are in <u>and</u> for the upcoming year as shown below. The categories can be modified.

Yr____	Patient Visits	New Patients	New PIs	Pt. Referrals	Resigns	Services	Total Coll.	Ins. Coll.	Pt. Coll.
Goal									

Yr____	Patient Visits	New Patients	New PIs	Pt. Referrals	Resigns	Services	Total Coll.	Ins. Coll.	Pt. Coll.
Goal									

Fill in your goals for the first two years after opening. Once again, this requires thinking. If you get stuck just call me. I will guide you right!

Once our yearly goal numbers have been correctly engineered (and it is harder than it looks) we divide them by 12 to get our monthly goals. We then divide the yearly numbers by 50 to get our weekly goals.

As mentioned, we actually have a printed guide on how to do this along with several videos of me teaching this process precisely. Once this is learned, a doctor can prosper from this tool for decades.

There is nothing more important when starting out than having clear, accurate, smart, and complete goals. <u>Once clear goals are set then everything you do from that point on is moving you towards them.</u>

We make sure all our clients have clear thoughts and complete goals. Our members routinely break their records and have to reset their goals time and time again. This is what makes practice fun and rewarding.

You be the Coach:

A chiropractor hires you to be their consultant. You say to her: *Send me your goals for your first year.* She sends you this:

Yr 20XX	Patient Visits	New Patients	Pt. Referrals	Resigns	Services	Total Coll.
Goal	10,000	400	150	100	$1,000,000	$900,000

What do you tell her?

How much will she have to collect per visit to reach this?

What will her case average need to be for this collection goal?

How many new DCs do you think have ever collected $900,000 their first year open?

My answer: Clearly this doctor is excited and ready to go, but we must get her mind <u>accurate</u> and create goals that make mathematical sense. To collect $900,000 in year one is virtually impossible. I am not sure if it has ever been done more than a handful of times in history. Remember there is a ramping up phase that takes a few months even for the best veterans. This doctor wanted to argue with me saying: *I can set any goals I want!*

Yes, we can set any goals we want as long as they are smart and accurate. <u>Accurate thinking</u> is one of the laws of success.

According to the above numbers, to achieve $900,000 a year in collections would mean she would have to collect $90 per visit. I have never seen a DC collect $90 per visit in her state.

We corrected the numbers and sure enough she had a great first year collecting over $250,000. Then broke her records the following year!

I realize you are not exactly sure how all the numbers work and what smart or accurate goals are just yet. You are also not certain on what stats to track. You must be taught this by an expert.

Every successful business tracks everything. Often down to the hundredth of a second and certainly down to the dollar. A successful chiropractic office is no different. You are starting a <u>real business</u>.

Too many doctors start what amounts to be a lemonade stand level business. When they struggle, hopefully they will call me. We will fix everything so they can own a real business. They will then be able to grow and enjoy the level of practice, and life, a chiropractor deserves.

Many doctors think they are "too smart" to hire an expert consultant. After not doing well year after year they say they "can't afford" to hire a coach. It is hard to help people who cannot think successfully.

The real PRO wastes no time trying to figure things out on their own. The PRO immediately buys the knowledge of others and uses it. This is the most efficient way to prosper while those "too smart" or "too cheap" to join the group end up underproducing and frustrated.

Remember, we never defend what is not working. I have had doctors argue with me about how good their systems and procedures are, even though they are barely able to pay their bills. Some will defend their money flow system yet they are behind on their taxes.

If you are willing to pay the price and work hard, you may become a chiropractic champion. If you are not willing to put forth the time, effort, and money required… then forget it.

Unless another doctor is doing REALLY WELL based on real numbers (and not based on how well they "look" like they are doing), we probably should not take any practice success advice from them. In other words, we only take advice from those who are truly winning!

You may not believe this, but some people don't want to win. Some are not able to see the better way. Some are wired or simply programmed to be average. For these people, anything they are exposed to that is above their level of thinking they automatically reject.

Our entire program is designed to make every doctor and team MUCH more successful than they would be on their own. Success is learned. You must learn it. Which means you must pay to learn it. Which means someone has to have the delivery systems to teach it to you.

Key Goal and Stat Terms to Understand:

Patient Visits:

>The total number of people you adjusted including family and friends. We normally only count them if performed in the office. It is an incredibly foolish habit to adjust anyone outside your office. Get them in your office where you are at your best.

>Note: Your malpractice insurance only covers you in the state you practice in. If you adjust anyone while outside your home state

you are not covered if anything happens. Most doctors do not know this.

The goal here is to hit 100 visits per week within 90 days of opening. The next goal is 50 patients per day and up from there.

New Patients:

Anyone who comes in the office and receives an exam is considered a new patient whether they start care or not. A human being can only be a new patient in your office once in their lifetime. Even if this person vanishes then comes back years later for an exam they are considered a reactivated patient.

A new patient goal starting out should be at least 30 new patients per month but 50 or more is better. Moving to Minneapolis I had 93 new patients my first month. With the right goals, vision, intention, systems, and plan you can do it too!

New PIs:

Many offices track and have goals for Personal Injury patients. This is anyone injured in an automobile crash. Motorcycle, snowmobile, and watercraft injures are covered much differently, if at all. Commonly, personal injury auto cases pay well as they are more complex. A good goal here is 1-5 cases per month.

Patient Referrals:

Any new patient that was directly referred to you by a current or past patient. These are commonly the best new patients as they have already heard good things about you. They are also the least expensive. They cost nothing to get compared to a marketed new patient. A goal here is to have at least half your NPs be referrals.

Re-signs:

A patient that decides to continue care with you after their initial care plan. There is an art to Re-signing patients. We have probably the best system ever devised for chiropractors to get patients to stay under care for years. 100 Re-signs your first year is a smart goal. One of my clients had 57 Re-signs last month.

Services:

This is the total dollar amount of the services you provided using retail fees. This is sometimes called total charges. We will need to determine a smart goal here for you as it will differ from state to state. As a general rule, this should be 20% higher than your collection goal.

Total Collections:

The total amount collected including any insurance money, cash payments, payments from attorneys, collections for supplements. Include everything! This is always a % of the services provided. We will create a smart goal here. A goal to collect $250,000 the first year is an excellent reference point.

Insurance Collections:

The amount collected from all insurance companies.

Cash Collections:

The amount collected directly from patients.

PVA:

This is your Patient Visit Average. It is better and more descriptively known as **Retention**. How good are you at keeping patients? How much do people like coming in to see you? PVA along with patient referrals are the two most important stats that tell a doctor how well they are doing.

It takes at least 6 months of numbers to calculate an accurate PVA.

PVA = Total Visits / New Patients

A good number to seek is a PVA of 24+. Many DCs like myself have a PVA well over 100.

Doctor 1: This doctor gets 10 new patients and has a PVA of 14 visits. This means the typical patient sees them 14 times then disappears. 10 new ones x 14 visits = 140 total patient visits

At $40 collected per visit this doctor collects $40 x 140 = **$5600.**

Doctor 2: This doctor gets the same 10 new patients but has much better coaching, image, layout, a more likable personality, a more capable CA, and smarter payment arrangements. They have a PVA of 42. So: 10 new ones x 42 visits = 420 total patient visits for this doctor.

At $40 collected per visit, this doctor gets $40 x 420 = **$16,800.**

Would you rather be $5600 doctor or the $16,800 doctor?

PVA is KING! Many doctors cannot get people to stay with them for countless reasons. They are forced to do a lot of marketing in an attempt to replace those that patients that quit.

The most successful doctors have a TON of patients who love to come see them one, two, three, or four times every month for years. This is what it is all about. We want as many people as possible to benefit from chiropractic care forever!

Case Average:

The average amount you collect on every new case/patient. In some businesses this may be called the average revenue per customer or average total amount spent per customer over time.

It is the Total Collections / New Patients.

Example: Over a year you collect $525,000 and had 375 new patients that year. $525,000 / 375 = $1400 Case Average.

A good Case Average is $1500 or more.

Services Per Visit:

The average dollar amount of services per visit, using retail fees, provided to patients.

Take the Total Services / Total Visits = Services Per Visit.

Total Services $480,000 / 6700 visits = $72 in Services Per Visit.

Collections Per Visit:

Total Collections / Total Visits = Collection Per Visit. A critical stat that must be watched every month. Ideally this number should be greater than the fee for your 98940.

Doctor 1: This doctor saw 475 visits last month and had total collections of $27,814. $27,814 / 475 = **$58.55** collected per visit.

Doctor 2: This doctor saw 820 visits with total collections of $24,237. $24,237 / 820 = **$29.56** collected per visit.

Notice Doctor 2 saw 345 <u>more</u> visits than Doctor 1 but collected <u>less</u> money. What does this mean?

Are you starting to see that goals, stats, and all elements of clinic operations are not only interesting but incredibly important?

Collection %:

How much of the services you provided did you actually collect? Total Collections / Total services = % Collections.

Example: Collections $77,876 / Services $102,593 = 76%   This doctor collected 76% of all the services they provided this month.

This may be good <u>or bad</u> depending on what this doctor's average is. If they normally collect 85% of their services then this must be analyzed to find out why it dropped.

Final Word on Vision and Intention:

You must understand how all the numbers work in YOUR practice!

You be the Coach:

A DC asks you: *Hey, what do you think about me going all cash?*

Your answer?

My answer: *What if you have a friend who is a cash patient and they get in an accident and are now covered 100% for care? Are you going to tell them they still have to pay, or go someplace else?*

What if you have a great cash patient that turns 65 and is now covered by Medicare, are you going to tell them to go someplace else? Your brother is hurt at work and is covered 100% for 12 weeks, are you going to try to charge him cash or send him somewhere else?

It is my official coaching opinion that every DC should be an absolute expert with <u>all 5 types of patients</u>. Auto injury, work injury, Medicare, cash, and regular insurance. The PRO chiropractor knows how to expertly handle every patient that walks through their door.

New grad: *Tory, where do I get the money to start a practice?*

Consultant: *Uh... you tell me.*

New grad: *Well I don't know.*

Consultant: *What have you been thinking about the last three and a half years? Let me get this right: You sat in chiropractic college for 3 and a half years, knowing graduation was coming and that you wanted to open an office, and in all that time you didn't think about what your options were to get the money to start?*

New grad: *Well I was focused on school and Boards.*

Consultant: *Yeah, so was everybody else. Including the ones who already have their money and practice plan figured out.*

New grad: *I know but now I need to.*

Consultant: *Yes, you are right.* **YOU** *do need to get after it. How would I know what your options are? I have no idea what you already have for money, no idea who your family is, no idea of your credit rating, no idea what your monthly costs to live are, no idea if you are married, no idea if you have kids, no idea where you want to go, no idea how much it will cost you to open, and no idea who you may know that might give you a loan. How would I possibly know where YOU can get any money?*

This example may seem a bit snippy but I wanted to illustrate a point. People can be physically lazy. They can also be mentally lazy.

Some are unable or unwilling to "think" and work with their mind to figure things out. The super success in any field is the person who can sit alone at a desk and THINK.

The ability to think hard, make lists of options, draw things out, calculate things, plan, sketch, process ideas, ponder the future, and see multiple scenarios playing out used to be

Another view of what success looks like. You must be able to sit alone and think, figure things out, and plan.

All great ideas happen when you are alone and in the silence.

common sense. Today it is literally a superpower as so few can do it. Can you?

The way you must be able to think NOW is completely different than the way you have "thought" your entire life.

We teach that YOU need to sit and do some thinking <u>first</u>. Once YOU have YOUR ideas as complete and as smart as YOU can get them, only then do you go to the expert and say: *I put together these ideas on how to get some money to start my practice, what do you think?*

It is not anyone else's job to help a new doctor figure out how to secure funds. It is a personal endeavor that must be accomplished.

Here are some possible angles to secure money to start a practice. Listed from simplest and most fortunate to bootstrapping.

Where to get money:

- Just use all the money you have saved your entire life and self-fund your new office.
- Ask parents or another family member to simply give you the money to start your new office.
- Take $150,000 of an inheritance early to start your business.
- Have parents or a family member give you a personal loan with terms to pay it all back to them directly.
- Have a family member get a home equity loan for you to use, then you make the payments back to the bank.
- Have a family member co-sign a loan that you need to pay back.
- Get a loan from a non-family investor then pay it back.
- Take out the max loans in school. Don't use it all and save as much as possible for practice start-up.
- Work through school and save as much as you can to be ready to start your business.
- Get as many credit cards as possible with as large of limits as possible. Using credit cards to start is no different than any other loan, you are borrowing from a bank either way.

- If married, it's possible the spouse has money, income, or family that may co-sign a loan or help.
- Any combination of the above. Whatever it takes to get it done!

Examples:

- A new grad has a surgeon dad who builds her a new office just the way she wants it and gives her money to get going.
- A new DC has nothing and starts with $6000 that he had available on two credit cards.
- Personally, my grandmother secured a $36,000 home equity loan for me. I paid back every penny. This was incredibly generous as she never could have paid it back on her own.
- One client took $200,000 of his inheritance early and used it to get started.
- Another doctor had $20,000 saved, had a couple credit cards with a total of $15,000 available, and was able to get a family loan for $50,000. This doctor had a total of $85,000 to start.
- A DC and his wife have $15,000 saved, $10,000 of credit card availability, and are able to get a family member to co-sign an SBA loan for $75,000.
- A doctor had $2000, another $10,000 in credit card availability, and a family loan for $20,000. They negotiated and got the landlord to finance the buildout and add it into the lease.

The key here is that **you** have to look everywhere in **your** life and figure out a way! I can only help you <u>after</u> you let me know what your actual options are.

It is truly amazing how chiropractors start and succeed with so little money. To give you an idea: A popular fitness franchise requires $330,000 to $600,000 to open. A new franchisee must have all the money required to open plus an extra $100,000 in cash <u>just for marketing</u>. This is in the same square footage a typical chiropractor would use.

They have more money set aside for marketing alone than the chiropractor has to build, buy, and do <u>everything</u>! Our ability to start and succeed with so little makes us awesome!

How to Ask for Money:

Not smart example:

- *Hey, I need to borrow some money.*

Smart example:

- *I have a great location and have worked out all the lease details. I have already engineered and drawn to scale a great floor plan. I have a complete list room by room of all needed equipment. My promotion plan is ready to attract the new patients to be profitable immediately. I have also hired a proven practice success expert to guide me the entire way. I would like to borrow $50,000 which I will pay back with these terms:*

  Three months after opening I will auto-pay you $500 per month for the first 12 months followed by $1062 per month for the remaining 48 months. This represents a 6% return. I would like a provision to be able to pay it off early at any time with no penalty if that's okay?

The key point related to borrowing money, or lending money is that <u>you create the terms</u> that will work for everyone! You don't ask what the terms could be. You already have several options written down.

By showing you have thought things through proves you are smart. It also shows that you care about <u>them</u> and not just yourself. The goal is to inspire those you ask want to follow your ideas.

Business Plans:

You can look online for many examples of business plans. We have many members who will share theirs. We also recommend not creating anything though until you find out exactly what a lender wants.

How Much Money Do I Need:

As much as you can get. The general answer is $100,000 or more if possible. The goal is to get as much money to start as you can, then not need it all!

Questions:

- What is the most expensive component to opening a practice?
- What nearly always costs more than any other single thing?

Answer:

- The buildout or tenant improvements (TI) of the space is by far the most expensive element. This includes the walls, doors, carpet, paint, front desk, electrical, plumbing, and everything else required to bring all your equipment and systems in.

I know what you are thinking. You are thinking that you are a chiropractor and that "other people" will handle all the things you are clueless about. Wrong! YOU must now become an expert in everything.

You are now a business owner. This means you must learn everything possible about everything relating to your business. Leases, floor plans, dealing with contractors, vendors, utility companies, website design, marketing plans, patient management, hiring, firing, all accounting, and 1000 more things if you want to be successful.

Understand that chiropractic is simply your profession. It is only one small part of the many responsibilities you now need to be good at.

Many new doctors suffer here. They say things like: *I don't know anything about this,* or *I'm not very good at stuff like that.*

Not anymore! You must get good in a hurry because no doctor has the money to hire people to do everything for them. Though hiring me as your consultant is a good idea, I can't move to your city for 3 months and do it all for you even though I would love to!

Those who want to be the best are those who want to learn everything they can about being successful in their profession. Technique and patient care are only a small part of this.

You are a business owner, which requires you to become a business expert. The service being delivered within your business is chiropractic, which requires you to also become a chiropractic expert. You have two different skill sets to be excited about! I LOVE being a business owner and I LOVE being a chiropractor!

You Are Three People Now:

1. You are a **Promoter and Marketer** of chiropractic, your office, your care and yourself.

2. You are a **Practicing Chiropractor** and the manager of all things, services and people in your office.

3. You are a **Business Person**. A Businessman or Businesswoman.

Those who are the best <u>at all three</u> become the most successful chiropractors in the world. The cool thing is that most of this can be <u>learned</u>. You simply have to be willing to <u>learn</u> and apply smart information, like the super successful men and women did before you.

You be the Coach:

A doctor joins WINNERSEDGE and is now collecting more money. They have a surplus in their clinic checking account.

Question: *Hey coach what should I do with this extra $5000 I have in my business account? Should I invest it?*

You discover they have a practice loan for $20,000 but are not making any payments on it.

You ask: *Why is there no monthly payment to this practice loan?*

They reply: *Oh, that is from a family member who said I could pay it back whenever I wanted.*

Your coaching response would be?

My answer: *Let's right now set the terms to pay back that loan. We will automate the payments immediately. We create smart terms for all debt and never wait to pay back anything. It was a little sloppy to not have this planned out initially, but now we can get it on track!*

Once this is in place, then we can look at what is next in your debt elimination and wealth creation strategy.

Thanksgiving dinner feels a lot different when you owe someone at the table money. We want to pay loans like this right away. We prioritize family, never put them on the backburner.

Result: This doctor had the $20,000 paid back in full within four months. He said his mom cried when he made the last payment because she was so proud of her son for be so responsible.

Location gets a lot of attention because it is the most obvious component of starting a practice. Location, location, location is the cry of the real estate world. This is certainly true for some businesses and for homes, but not so much for the chiropractor. You are a destination location, not so much a visibility dependent operation like an ice cream shop or fast food place. Though we will take all the visibility we can get.

In its simplest sense, you pick your new office space from the best spaces available to rent in your area. It really is that easy. Yet at the same time it is infinitely complex and every scenario is different. This makes it difficult to even talk about. To discuss this properly we would need all YOUR available options on the table.

Thoughts on Location:

- Nobody can tell you where you should go.

- Nobody can tell you what YOU want or what YOU like.

- If after 3+ years in school upon graduation you are asking people: *Where is a good place to go?* You are already lost.

- ALL places might be good if you like the area.

- Go where you want to live and build a life for <u>many years.</u>

- I recommend living very close to the office for many reasons.

- What practice type do you want? Pure chiropractic, open adjusting, Gonstead, etc. This determines space requirements.

- You don't get to choose, you must pick from what is available.

- No space has everything, it just has to work well enough that you can be there for a long time.

- Moving an office is very expensive, just trying to get your address changed with everyone is hard. Go where you want to end up, even if you have to scrape to do it.

- Where you rent space is totally dependent on how much money you have, the current economics, and what is out there.

- Going where you know the most people is by far the best for getting new patients and creating income.

There Are Five Basic Types of Space:

The types of space available to you will vary based on how urban or rural your area is. I have seen a doctor buy a building in their small town of 1200 people for a great deal. I have also seen a doctor in the city rent space on the 4th floor of an office building that has 1200 people in it. Both can work great – if YOU like it!

You are going to be spending a third of your LIFE in this place, so get it where you want it. We put the office in the best spot for an office. Where you live is a different story. Notice, they never position a McDonalds where it will be convenient for the owner. It goes where it has the best chance of success. Same is true for you.

This isn't to say that we don't worry about where we will live. I recommend you carefully scope-out all the areas you may want to end up living. The combination of a great office location and great living location is THE foundation for a great life.

Build Your Own Building:

This was common decades ago. It happens much less today for many reasons. In some areas this can be feasible. I really like this if a smart opportunity presents itself.

Retail Space:

This is the classic chiropractic location in a strip mall or other ground level retail type scene. This is the easiest to find, most common to look for, and most expensive type of space. Visibility can be great here, but I have never seen visibility matter that much if at all.

My last office. A typical two-level retail space with very nice visibility but expensive. My truck, the only car in the lot again. The discipline to work hard vs. seek leisure is what creates a truly great practice and chiropractic power life!

I have had offices on roads with 50,000 cars driving by every day. I am now in a warehouse that you can't even see from the road. You build a following of people to come to you. You just have to be easy to find, have good parking, and a clear path to the front door.

Office Space:

This is usually a space inside an office building possibly on an upper floor. I have a great chiropractor friend who is on the second floor of an office building utilizing an "office" space. Because there are many tenants sharing costs on the same pad of concrete, normally this is less expensive. Any space not on ground level will also usually be less expensive.

If you can park close and get in the building easily then office space works. Plus, you can market to all the people in the building.

If there is a parking ramp across the street and patients have to walk 100 yards outside in the winter, then take the stairs three flights up, forget it. In any location it must be EASY for people to roll in and out from whatever direction they may come from.

Many doctors never think to look for office type space because they are so busy combing the strip malls for a potentially overpriced one that has no parking when you need it.

The DC super success surveys ALL possible spaces in their area. They then talk to me and we examine all the attributes and numbers so we can make the best decision and blast into action!

Showroom Space:

This type of space is designed to have a showroom area up front and a warehouse, manufacturing or storage in the back. Commonly with a garage door or a loading dock. An example is a carpet store or a paint store with displays and sales up front with a storage area in the back.

The picture I showed earlier with me kneeling next to the car was considered showroom space. I had the garage door removed and windows installed. I then used it as my chiropractic office. It was a great office in a great location.

Warehouse or Industrial Space:

A true warehouse space is just that - a building or space used for storage. It has no people working in it. Sometimes a warehouse or industrial space will be more versatile. It can have manufacturing, some offices, room for storage, and whatever else.

My current office started as a huge open warehouse with no air conditioning and two ratty bathrooms. I designed everything. The result is a perfect 1800 ft. chiropractic and consulting office with the 9200 ft. gym accessed through a set of double doors.

My current office. Plain and much more industrial in style. Less flashy but is functionally perfect and much less cost. I wonder whose car is the only one in the lot again? Up early in the cold preparing to change more lives!

What I have created here is something to see. Most doctors who visit cannot wrap their mind around all that is happening here and how impressive it is. This is the tangible result of some very hard mental work and visualization.

To give you an idea, my last space was $31 per ft. or around $4000 per month. (I will explain how all these numbers work in a minute.) The industrial space I am in now is less than 3 minutes away, is much better, and costs only $14 per ft. Under normal circumstance this would save $300,000 in rent over the next 10 years. Easily enough to pay student loans off early!

I have done something very unique for my clients. I have two videos of me personally building each of my last two offices from scratch. The plans, framing, electrical needs, front desk requirements, X-ray room requirements, paint colors, the best carpet to get, what type of lighting to use, where you need outlets, and more.

There are many details. What you should be doing while it is being built. How to deal with builders, vendors, and everything else needed to go from a bare floor to being able to open. We are not aware of anyone who has videos like this for the new doctor to watch and learn from. They are priceless if you want to open your own successful office.

How to Find an Office Space:

1. Drive around and look for all *For Lease* signs and call them.

2. Go to *loopnet.com* and look online there. This will not have every space but can still be super valuable. Especially if you are not in the town you want to go to and need to look online.

3. Hire a leasing agent. This is a last resort. They cost the potential landlord a LOT of money, you pay them nothing. They get paid a commission on the total value of a lease if they bring a landlord a new tenant.

    Example: Say a lease is $20 per ft. on 1200 ft. over 5 years. The total value of the lease is 20 x 1200 x 5 = $120,000. If the agent gets a 6% commission, the landlord now owes the leasing agent $7200 for bringing them a tenant.

    The Landlord would much rather deal with you directly. They may even give you more incentives to rent in place of paying the money to a leasing agent.

Now Let's Summarize the Basic Sequence of Events:

1. Join consulting group within a year of graduating.
2. Pass boards and graduate.
3. Get state license.
4. Find space and sign lease.
5. Start building out the space.
6. Get clinic name, banking, legal elements in order.
7. Furnish office with all equipment, chairs, posters etc.
8. Create and install all forms, computers, and office systems.
9. Engineer money flow and debt elimination strategy.
10. Fire up website and all social media.
11. Engage our *90 Day Practice Explosion* marketing plan.
12. Obtain Certificate of Occupancy from the city.
13. Open and hire team when ready.
14. Love people and get to 100 a week as fast as possible.
15. Then 50 patients a day.
16. Then 200 a week.
17. Then 75 a day.
18. Then 300 a week.
19. Then 100 patients a day growing to 200 a day if you desire.
20. Maintain ongoing training and seminars to stay sharp.

Are you an ultra-succeeder who wants to make a **SERIOUS DIFFERENCE** in your community and in the world?

The line I want you to remember when dealing with any potential landlord or their leasing agent is this (and only say it if you are serious about a potential space): *I am looking to be a good long-term tenant.*

This is music to their ears. Every landlord is hoping for good long-term tenants. If you were a landlord you would too.

Usually the doctor is so into their own project and their own "needs" they are unable to think about anything other than themselves. To be successful you need to put yourself in other people's shoes. Think about what they want and use this information successfully.

I am neither a real estate attorney nor a highly trained real estate expert. The following is what I know from personal experience as a landlord and as a tenant. I recommend you consult other experts for any specific questions or situations that may require it. I certainly have many times.

What Landlords Want:

- Good tenants who pay on time.

- Quiet tenants that don't bother anyone in or outside the property.

- Tenants whose business benefits the other tenants on the property.

- Clean tenants who take nice care of and have pride in their space.

- Tenants who renew their lease and stay forever.

- Tenants who don't call and whine all the time.

- Tenants who know their responsibility and don't try to get the landlord to do what they should be handling themselves.

Key Lease Language to Understand:

Term:

> The length of the lease. Usually 5 years but some are as low as 3 or as much as 7 or even 10 years. Landlords normally like longer leases. Sometimes we can get a little better deal if you sign a longer lease. The term is a negotiable item.

Base Rent:

The rent due, <u>not</u> including any other costs of the space. This is normally given per square foot. Like $14 per ft. or $29 per ft. Base rent is negotiable.

Example 1: Say a space is $19 per ft. per <u>year</u> and has 1200 rentable feet. 19 x 1200 = $22,800 per year or $1900 per month.

Example 2: In some states it may be $2 per ft. per <u>month</u>. If the space is 1200 ft. you owe 2 x 1200 = $2400 per month.

Base rent is only part of what you will pay each month. The key is for you to look at all the costs and figure out what you will <u>actually have to write the check for</u> each month.

CAM:

Common Area Maintenance. This is the cost of lawn care, shoveling, window cleaning, garbage removal, parking lot lights, etc. that the tenant will benefit from. The tenant occupies only a percentage of the building therefore only pays their due percentage of CAM.

CAM is usually estimated, then at the end of the year they see if they were accurate. You may still owe more or get some money back if the CAM was less than what they collected for it. (Though it is rare that a landlord will let tenants know if they estimated high and actually owe the tenants money.)

This is normally stated like: $4.35 per ft. So if you are renting 1200 ft. the CAM will be 4.35 x 1200 = $5220 per year, breaking down to $435 per month for CAM. CAM is not negotiable, but make sure you are only paying your due percentage.

Tax:

All properties pay property taxes. Again, this is paid based on the percentage of the building a tenant occupies. Not negotiable. Taxes are what they are.

Tax is given just like CAM. For example: $7.15 per ft. for tax. If you are renting 1400 ft. you will owe 7.15 x 1400 = $10,010 a year or $834 per month for tax.

<u>TI:</u>

Tenant Improvements. This means what it says. When you hear the term TI, it also means how much money the landlord is willing to give the tenant to help build out the space. TI can be zero dollars up to a complete turn key buildout. This is negotiable.

Again, this depends on the total amount of rent to be paid by the tenant. If a tenant is going to pay $490,000 over 5 years for a lease then a landlord could possibly give $80,000 in TI.

<u>Buildout Allowance:</u>

Same as TI. The buildout allowance is what the landlord will provide financially to help a tenant prepare the space to occupy. This can be stated in a per foot or a flat amount basis.

Example: TI is $15 per ft. on a 1200 ft. space. This means you will get 15 x 1200 = $18,000 from the landlord.

Example: The landlord says they will give you a flat $24,000 in improvement money.

Know that in almost all cases you have to pay for all the improvements and buildout <u>first</u>. Then after all contractors and subcontractors are fully paid will the landlord then release a check back to you for the allowance.

<u>Vanilla Shell:</u>

This is a space that has drywall on the inside and sometimes basic lighting, HVAC, and a bathroom.

<u>Grey Shell:</u>

Sometimes called a cold shell. Concrete or unfinished walls, no lights, no bathroom, nothing. By far the most expensive to build out since it needs everything.

<u>HVAC:</u>

Heating Ventilation and Air Conditioning. Seems simple but in commercial space HVAC is a big deal. There can be a shared or individual HVAC unit. There may be a fee to maintain it. Keeping a space evenly warm or cool takes some engineering.

Turn Key:

A space that is completely built out by the landlord and ready to move in for the tenant. I have never seen this personally but it can happen in some areas under certain economic conditions.

Triple Net Lease (NNN):

A lease deal where the tenant pays the base rent, the CAM, and the tax. All three are paid in full by the tenant so the landlord has zero net cost for owning the space being rented.

Certificate of Occupancy:

Many cities give a Certificate of Occupancy or a business license once the buildout is done and has passed any required inspections. You cannot operate until the city says it is okay.

Bumps:

The term used to describe how much the rent will go up each year. Normally it's a percentage of about 3%. In fact, anything over 3% will be a problem. This is negotiable.

Business Insurance:

You will have a business insurance policy that will cover everything inside the space and any damage to anything inside the premises. The landlord will have a policy that covers everything outside the walls of your space.

SAC:

Sewer Access Charge. A fee by the city for a business to access the sewer. Normally not an issue for chiropractors.

The gym in my space wants showers. A great idea until we discover that the City of Eden Prairie demands a $15,000 SAC fee per shower to access the sewer with the shower drains.

So, one men's and one women's shower would be $30,000 just for the permit. This is why most small gyms do not have showers.

Usable Square Feet:

The amount of space you can actually occupy and utilize for your business. The square footage inside the four walls of your space not including any common or shared areas.

Common Area:

An area that multiple tenants may share. This can be an entryway, restrooms that serve multiple offices, hallways, elevators, or various other areas.

If you have access to or use the space even rarely you will probably have to pay for it. Notice you may only have a space that is 1200 ft. but when you add in the common areas you may be responsible to pay rent for 1300 ft.

Rentable Square Feet:

Usable ft. + Common areas = Rentable ft. This is the amount of square footage you are responsible to pay for.

Considerations for Space:

How much do I write the check for each month?

The Base rent + the CAM + the Tax = Total cost per ft. rented.

Example:	Base rent	$14.50
	CAM	$ 3.75
	Tax	$ 5.50
	Total	$23.75 per ft.

Rentable square feet of space: 1235 ft.

So: $23.75 x 1235 ft. = $29,331.50 per year

$29,331.50 / 12 months = $2444.27 per month

There are occasions where it is very simple. A landlord may just charge $1500 per month all in, meaning the CAM, tax, and sometimes even utilities are included in the $1500. This is nice, but not too common.

<u>Buildout cost vs. How much $ you have:</u>

Building out the office is normally the most expensive part of getting started. This can range from nothing to over $100,000 depending on what you are starting with, how fancy your office is, and how much the landlord will help financially if at all.

You must determine how much total money you can secure, then consider the cost to prepare the space. As a general rule you need twice as much as what it will cost to build out the space.

Determining the cost to build out a space requires an accurate plan drawn by you, then given to a contractor to make a rough bid.

We do not get any contractor involved if we don't feel we are ready to roll. You never want to waste anyone's time.

If the space is a vanilla shell and you only have $50,000 and the landlord offers no TI money, then this space will probably not work because you can't afford it. A vanilla shell will almost certainly cost over $50,000 to build out, so you will need to find a different space or somehow get more money.

<u>What does it *feel* like?</u>

When considering a space, we recommend you drive there from <u>all</u> directions. What does it *feel* like? Then sit in the parking lot and look at the building and all the surroundings. What does that *feel* like? Walk around the parking lot and building. What does it *feel* like? If you can get in the space. Stand inside it - what does it *feel* like?

Listen to your subconscious mind. Listen to your innate. How an area and a space *feels* is important. If it does not *feel* good then determine why. Do this with all potential spaces.

<u>What is next to you?</u>

Is the space you are looking for next to a fitness center that hogs all the parking spots when you need them most? Is it next to a fast food restaurant, fish market, or a pizza place that is going to smell-up your office every day?

Is it next to a business that can work well for referrals? Is it next to a space that might be loud or have things banging the walls? I had an office next to a tanning salon that cranked their hip hop music every day and annoyed us like crazy. I had an office next to a space where they hit the walls so hard it cracked my drywall.

I had an office where suddenly water started pouring from the ceiling all over my adjusting table. The hair salon above us had their washing machine back up. It was fixed quickly so I wasn't overly mad. Hair salons send in a lot of patients.

You can't have everything perfect, but if you move next to a place that really annoys you, it is your own fault. If you are already there and a new tenant moves in, cross your fingers they are both pleasant and good for your business.

<u>Where is the sun?</u>

Most wouldn't think of this, but I always want to know how and when the sun comes through the windows. Does the space face north or south where the sun will hammer you in the afternoon?

The sun's position can be important for window shades, CA desk placement, and heating/air conditioning vents. I promise you if a CA is by the front door in Wisconsin in January they will be freezing and crank up the heat while the doctor in the back is burning up. You wouldn't think it now, but temperature control in an office is very important and must be planned correctly.

<u>Traffic in and out, Stoplights, Intersections:</u>

How easy is the location to get to? Is there a hairy intersection where everyone will have to sit forever waiting to turn?

The easier people can get to you and navigate your parking lot the better. If a patient is heading home from work and is in a hurry, unless you are easy to get to, they will just drive right by.

<u>Parking during primetime in all seasons:</u>

Does a potential space look great at 10am when you check it out only to be jammed with yoga people for a neighboring business at 5pm when you need parking for your patients?

Does the office look great but in the winter time the plow truck piles up snow which eats 10 parking spots making it so you and many of your patients have to park a block away and walk through slush to get to your door?

Our first job is to <u>think</u>. See and figure out as best you can what it will be like in ALL seasons at ALL times of day.

Signs, what kind are best and who pays for them?

Every building will have rules for signs. You can't just go make anything you want. Get any sign covenants <u>before</u> you have a sign made and installed. Normally this will be in the lease but sometimes it is a separate document.

You will pay for your sign. Some locations may have a small placard with your name on it which may be included on a monument sign for the entire building free of charge. Either way, you want the best signage the property will allow.

If you spend any significant money on a sign, make sure it is included in your insurance policy. Even though it is outside your space it can be covered. This is important as there are many ways an expensive sign can be damaged. I have paid $500 up to $9000 for a sign. A good clinic name, a good URL, a good logo and a good sign are all valuable.

Who pays the utilities?

Normally you pay for any electric, gas, water and sanitation. Sometimes in simpler leases these may be included in the rent.

What is a Letter of Intent?

A brief synopsis of the terms of a lease that you can sign to secure the space until a formal lease is executed. It gets you semi-obligated to the space and keeps the landlord from renting it to someone else.

You are not really bound until you have a fully signed lease.

What can I do to negotiate a better deal?

- You can try to get the base rent down a little.
- You can try to get more in tenant improvement money (TI).
- You can try to get a few free months of rent.

- You can attempt to go from a 3-year deal to a 5-year in exchange for two months free rent.
- You can negotiate to pay half the rent for 3 months.
- You can try to get them to pay for the buildout, then you pay the landlord back plus a % or flat amount of interest over the term of the lease. **For example:** A buildout costs $45,000. You agree to pay the landlord back $50,000 over the next 60 months of the lease in addition to the lease payment.

There are infinite possibilities that can occur. The demand for space in your area, how many units the landlord owns, and overall economic conditions will all come in to play.

Doing this right:

This is one of 100 reasons why you call me. We can go over all the details of your situation and make the right choices.

If you don't do this right the first time you will spend years paying for it. A mess up on space or layout is unbelievably expensive and very difficult to fix.

Imagine getting all set up in a great space with a great deal. We will create a great looking office that you, your team, and all your patients will love to be in!

We use live video *Zoom* calls so my clients can show me anything they have concerns about. It is like me being right next to them as they make career impacting decisions.

Remember an office is valuable. You are creating probably the most valuable thing you may ever own. A nice office with a timeless design is essential.

What is a practice worth anyway?

There are several ways a practice value can be determined. I feel it is important to know what you are building. There are experts such as *(practicebrokersinc.com)* we call to more accurately value practice if necessary for a purchase or a practice sale.

Very generally a practice is worth maybe 75% of the last 12 months collections. You would never use this method to actually buy or sell an office, it is simply the quickest general guide.

Example: You collected $425,000 over the last 12 months. 75% of $425,000 = $318,000.

A more detailed approach may call for the current garage sale value of everything in the office including the garbage cans, plus 35% of the accounts receivable that will actually be collected, plus the "Goodwill" of the practice. Goodwill consists of the last 12-months profit after all relevant expenses.

Example:

Equipment and all in the office:	$42,000
Collectible receivables x 35%:	$12,000
Goodwill - Last 12 mo. Profit:	$223,000
Practice value	$277,000

We make sure anything we build is as valuable as possible!

When do I need an attorney?

We recommend you always have a qualified local attorney review all leases before signing.

You must sit and carefully read every single word with a highlighter FIRST. Never be lazy and think someone else will be looking out for you. You are a serious business owner now, this means you read and understand every single word of any document that binds you to time and money.

Tory, I want to buy a practice:

Buying a practice is an incredibly complex project.

Phase 1: Preparing to buy.

Phase 2: The closing and transition.

Phase 3: The first 90 days you are in by yourself.

All three of these must be planned and handled perfectly. If not, you will have just bought something and allowed its value to sift through your fingertips leaving you with nothing but a big loan payment every month for years to come.

If you are looking to buy a practice call me immediately.

Rent negotiation examples:

Example 1:

A client of mine told me they found a nice space for a low price. They said: *Tory I have a great space and they want $1200 per month for a 3-year deal. How much do you think I should get from the landlord for buildout and tenant improvement money? I was going to ask for at least $40,000. What do you think?*

This doctor is about to be very embarrassed and prove to the potential landlord they have no idea how this works. In the $43,000 the building owner is going to collect in rent over the 3-year lease how can they possibly give you $40,000 of it for TI? In this case they can give you no improvement money.

Example 2:

Doctor says: *Hey, my landlord won't give me any improvement money, can I ask for anything else?*

Yes, ask for 3 months free rent. In this case, they got it and are a 100 patient a day office right now.

Example 3:

Proposed deal by landlord:

Base rent	$17.50
CAM	$ 3.95
Tax	$ 4.25
Bumps	5%
Term	3 years
TI	$5000
Usable feet	1350 ft.
Rentable feet	1525 ft.

Question: How much is owed each month in total rent?

Answer: 17.50 + 3.95 + 4.25 = $25.45 per ft.

$25.45 x 1525 = $39,192.50 / 12 = $3266 per month

Next question: What do you ask for to make this a better deal?

Answer: *Mr. Landlord, how about we go to $17 per foot, 3% Bumps, one month rent free, and I will do a 5-year deal? Mr. Landlord, I'd really like to preserve as much cash initially as I can for marketing, <u>I want to be a really good long-term tenant.</u>*

Result: The landlord agreed and this DC is ultra-successful today. The reason is because we did not just try to "get" or "take." Too many new people in business only try to "get get get" or "take take take." They always end up losing over time. You must GIVE. *What can I GIVE the landlord that will make them want to GIVE me something valuable in return?* We GAVE the landlord 2 more years, making it worth it for them to GIVE us a better deal.

Always remember the key language: *I want to be a really good long-term tenant.* This is music to a landlord's ears.

The most successful men and women anywhere are the ones who can create situations where <u>everyone wins</u>. Notice in this last example, the landlord wins, we win, the patients will win, the neighboring businesses will win, the bank will win, the equipment companies will win.

Go getters end up eating dirt. ***Go givers*** <u>prosper</u>. You must first give to the soil to get a harvest. Too many misguided, lied to, and often self-entitled people want to just take from the soil without giving any seeds or labor first.

Example 4:

<u>Proposed deal by landlord:</u>

Base rent	$14.75
CAM	$ 7.50
Tax	$ 3.25
Bumps	2%

Term	5 years
TI	None
Usable feet	1275 ft.
Rentable feet	1440 ft.

Question: How much is owed each month in total rent?

Answer: 14.75 + 7.50 + 3.25 = $25.50 per ft.

$25.50 x 1440 = $36,720 / 12 = $3060 per month

Question: Let's say the cost to build out the space and put up all the walls, doors, lighting, front desk, painting, ceiling tiles, and sprinkler heads will be around $50,000 <u>but</u> you only have $25,000 available for all the required improvements. What do you do?

Answer: *Mr. Landlord, I have an idea. I really want to be in this space and be a good long-term tenant. I agree to all your terms but how about: If I pay for $25,000 of the improvements would you be willing to pay the other $25,000 in improvements if I agree to pay you back $30,000 over the term of the lease?*

$30,000 / 60 months = $500 per month added to the lease = A new total rent of $3560 per month.

The landlord agreed and this office is very successful today!

I spend a lot of time fixing very costly lease, location, and layout mistakes. These must be avoided. Call me when it comes time to open your office. And of course, have an attorney read all leases before signing.

There are unlimited scenarios possible. Once you are looking at spaces we will consider all the best options for you. I really like the challenge of getting every doctor I meet into a great space with a great deal and a great layout. We will make sure you have an exceptional office in a location you love. The goal is to see thousands of people and create the chiropractic power life. Believe me, it's worth it!

Just because an office "looks" ready to open does not mean it actually "is" ready to open. All the invisible parts of the practice, along with all the legal elements must also be in place and ready.

- ❑ Certificate of Occupancy or local business license. (If required)
- ❑ Personal and Corporate NPI numbers on file.
- ❑ State license to practice chiropractic.
- ❑ Registration with your State Board of Chiropractic.
- ❑ EIN or your SS4 is on file.
- ❑ Registration with the Secretary of State.
- ❑ State ID# if needed in your state.
- ❑ Malpractice coverage in place. We recommend 2Mil/4Mil.
- ❑ Business insurance policy in place.
- ❑ Work Comp policy in place if starting with an employee.
- ❑ Fully executed and attorney reviewed lease in place.
- ❑ Business card, letterhead, and envelope set professionally made and stocked up. Our graphics people are who to call for this.

  You are out to create a brand: Name, logo, business card, website and office. Everything works together to create your own brand!

- ❑ Website created and complete. We have specific website criteria requirements and recommendations.
- ❑ All phone numbers, fax, and credit card lines working.
- ❑ All merchant processing systems up and working.
- ❑ Online automated payment system in place and working so you can receive automated payments from patients.
- ❑ Deposit stamps made for depositing checks.
- ❑ All bank accounts, debit cards, credit cards, and online banking in order and organized for both clinic and personal accounts.
- ❑ Payroll system, accounting system, and Sales and Use Tax payment system in place.
- ❑ In some states a Provider Tax is due, this system must be in place.

Additional elements to have ready:

- ❏ The clinic fee schedule must be complete with all CPT codes entered into the system.

- ❏ All forms customized, copied, in place, and ready. We have an incredible Forms Set for our clients. Great forms are priceless.

- ❏ The primary ICD-10 codes and code sets handy.

- ❏ Billing software and computer system, including any scanners and printers ready to go.

- ❏ All new patient and report scripting memorized. Make a video of them for analysis, then practice and be ready for your patients.

- ❏ A hanging file folder with referral packs for the local MRI center, Neurologist and/or Orthopedic expert. A busy office will get cases that need an MD eval. The PRO chiropractor is ready for this. (Every DC should get a tour of their local MRI center.)

- ❏ Wellness plans created and in place. We have these for our clients.

- ❏ Staff hours, pay structure, bonuses, vacation, sick days, seminar requirements and all employment information organized, with each employee having a file folder with their W4 and other legal documents required for employment.

- ❏ All loans have their own hanging file folder plus online account log-ins created for all debts. You clearly understand how each debt works and the plan to crush each one.

- ❏ Get a frequent flyer number for the most used airline in your area.

- ❏ Consider an alarm for the office. Thieves literally make an occupation of finding new businesses to steal TVs, laptops, computers, and printers from. They do this before the business owner is smart enough to have an alarm. My last two offices were both broken into. My alarm system auto-called me and the police right away saving us $$.

We have recommendations and resources for everything above and many other practice essentials beyond the scope of this book.

Preparing a small business and chiropractic office to open has many critical elements that must be in order to make a great start. Simply know that the right consultant can save you literally millions by helping to make sure this is all done correctly.

I personally know two doctors in prison right now because of these mistakes. They went ahead doing whatever "they wanted" without all the proper legal elements and systems in place.

You are being watched. Your State Board of Chiropractic, the Attorney General, IRS, Dept. of Revenue, Dept. of Commerce, every Insurance Company, and Medicare to name a few. Not to mention, there are chiropractors all around just waiting to turn you in for something.

You will graduate and be allowed to send and get paid directly from insurance companies <u>and</u> the US Government. This is a BIG DEAL. Who can do this? This is a <u>privilege</u>. A license to practice chiropractic is considered a PRIVILEGE. It is not a right you have. It is a privilege that can be taken away at any moment if you don't play by the rules.

There is no doing anything crafty or illegal that cannot be discovered <u>easily</u> by any investigator. **Integrity** is a pillar quality for success!

ALL new chiropractors MUST get a copy of their State Board Administrative Laws, Rules, Statutes, and Regulations regarding chiropractic.

Read <u>every single word</u> carefully. This is what you can and can't do. Herein lies the standard you are held to.

When a doctor asks me if something is "legal" or not, this is where you look first.

The PRO chiropractor does not guess if it is okay to do something. They research and know <u>before</u> they act.

Saying: *But I see other doctors are doing it* **means nothing. YOU are 100% responsible for everything YOU do.**

MODULE 7   *Layouts and Floorplans for The Future*

Starting Out You May Have:

1. An empty space to design and build from scratch.

2. An already built out space that will work with minor changes.

3. A space with walls that all need to be torn out.

Every space starts out differently. All we can do here is give general ideas. They may or may not apply to you until you know what you have to work with.

Remember our goal is to have the smallest, least expensive, best designed, coolest looking space possible that comfortably allows us to see as many patients as we are capable of.

Most chiropractic offices have a lousy design. I have now fixed so many I have lost track. Even with the crummiest design in the worst space imaginable, I can nearly always figure out how to make it work better. If not, we will want the doctor to move once their current lease ends, or even sooner if possible.

When you walk into a real WINNERSEDGE office you feel it. There are certain smart design cues that let you know you are in a serious clinic designed to help a TON of people in style.

Key Players in Building an Office:

Architect: Will need one to do a final drawing before a contractor can start building. Sometimes the contractor knows one. Sometimes you have to find a local one yourself.

Contractor: Person entrusted to coordinate the building of your office. Sometimes the landlord will recommend one, sometimes you have to find one, and sometimes you already know one.

Building Inspector: To build anything the contractor needs a permit. This permit then prompts inspectors to visit and make sure the work is done properly. Once any inspectors sign-off on the project, you can get a Certificate of Occupancy and be allowed to operate inside the space.

Electrician: Will do all lighting, outlets, light switches, lighted signs, special power for an X-ray machine plus any other electrical work.

Plumber: Sinks, bathrooms, water fountains, slop sinks, and utility sinks.

Ceiling Expert: For any drop or acoustical ceilings. A nice ceiling is essential. Many offices have dirty, droopy ceiling tiles. Never in a WINNERS**EDGE** office!

HVAC Expert: To make sure all heating, furnaces, air conditioning, humidifiers, thermostats, and fans all work well. Seems simple but temperature control is an entire science all its own.

Carpet and Flooring: Carpet, wood, laminate, or tile all are possible choices for a chiropractic office. Choosing these are a lot of fun. It is even more fun watching them be installed by an expert.

Framer: These people will put up all the wood or metal studs required for the walls. You must watch this process and make sure all the walls are exactly where they should be.

   With my first office I walked in and saw a main wall was off by exactly a foot. What a disaster this would have been if the rest of the walls would have been finished before I noticed.

   It is YOUR JOB to oversee and know everything! I cannot stress this enough. It is YOUR business. That means YOU have to look out for YOU and your project! Nobody else will.

Drywaller: These experts will take framed walls and make them real by putting up the drywall. Word of advice: *Never arm wrestle a drywaller!*

Mud and Taper: They will take the bare drywall walls and fill in all the corners, seams, cracks and get the walls smooth and ready to paint. This step is critical to having nice walls. Square framing + Well fitted drywall + Super flat and smooth mudding and taping + Good painting = A GREAT looking office. I now appreciate a nice smooth wall.

Painter: Well prepped and painted walls are a beautiful thing. This is a step that you could do yourself to save money but I don't recommend it.

Sign People: Will want to get this ordered quickly as it takes a few weeks to make most signs. Get whatever your landlord will allow. I always want to be there when the truck shows up to lift a new sign in to place! The instant your sign goes up everyone knows you are there! In the meanwhile, we recommend having a "Coming Soon" banner in the window.

Low Volt Specialist: These people install any phone lines, internet cables or other non-regular electrical stuff like alarm wiring, Wi-Fi, routers, cable, computers, and cameras.

Millwork Expert: This is who makes the counters for the front desk, plus any drawer systems, cupboards, and custom shelves. Your design and selections here are very important. The front desk can be the most expensive part of a buildout averaging $5000 to over $12,000 depending on its size and how many cabinets or drawer systems you want.

Designer: Not required but nice if you can find someone you like who does not cost too much. Here are the main things you will need to select. A designer can do all this if you have one.

- Paint colors: We recommend four paint colors and have criteria for choosing these. What color goes on what wall?

- Carpet and base trim: We recommend large carpet tiles and carpet base for sure. In certain climates wood, laminate or tile might be preferred.

- Laminate surfaces: This is the countertop and cabinet surfaces. Can be a flat color, woodgrain or any of endless choices and designs.

- Doors: Do you want grainy, dark, light, solid white, oak, maple, what? You get to pick.

- Door trim finishes: The trim color on the door frame for the wood or metal framed doors must be chosen.

- Light fixtures: We like what we call a "Blade" light for the CAs, cans with LEDs for the rooms, and nice bright lighting for any open reception or hot seat area. Plus we always want at least three wall sconces and cool pendant lights at the front desk hanging from a soffit.

- Another design element we like is a four-light switch panel. One switch for the CA lights, one for the open area, one for the sconces, and one for the pendants over the front desk.

- <u>Shades:</u> In offices we want mini blinds up front. We also mirror the front door so people cannot see in.

- Add any other design elements like posters, internal graphics, signs, or even cool murals for kids that are custom painted on the wall by an artist. Whatever you like!

Occasionally on a weekend I get special visitors in my office! Girl Daphny below and boy Indy to the right. My purebred European Dobermans. Notice below on the floor behind me carpet samples for a new office I was building.

Key point: With love and effort, dogs will grow up big and strong and love you. So will your practice <u>if you put love and effort into it.</u> I mean really love the easy and hard tasks required to make it great. LOVE your practice and it will LOVE you!

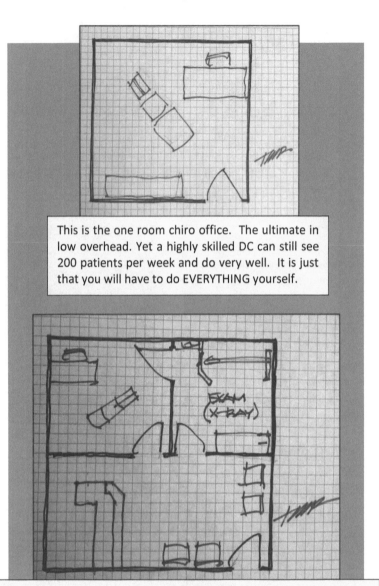

This is the one room chiro office. The ultimate in low overhead. Yet a highly skilled DC can still see 200 patients per week and do very well. It is just that you will have to do EVERYTHING yourself.

This is the very sweet 3 room office. DC Command Center, Exam/X-ray/ second adjusting room. A nice front desk and room for chairs. In my opinion this is the office of the future. It allows for maximum volume with the lowest overhead and most comfort. It may look simple but there are a LOT of smart design elements going on here that would take pages to explain. **Example:** Notice how the DC can sit at their desk in the top left corner and through a mirrored door be able see every person who walks in. I try to create this in all designs. It is great to know who just walked in so you can mentally prepare to deliver your best.

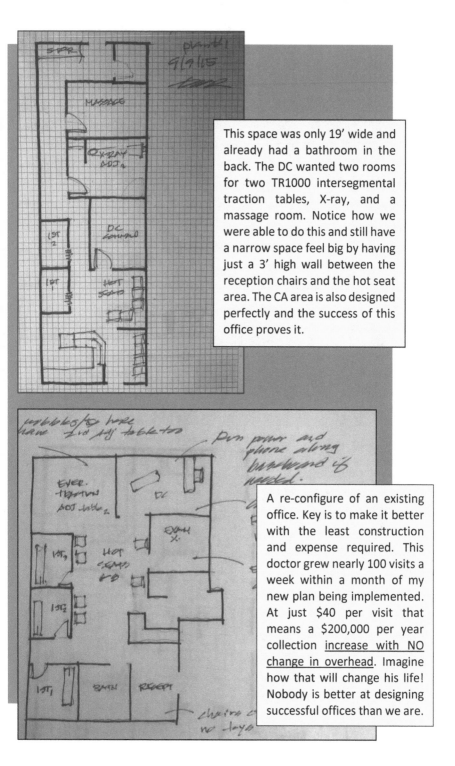

This space was only 19' wide and already had a bathroom in the back. The DC wanted two rooms for two TR1000 intersegmental traction tables, X-ray, and a massage room. Notice how we were able to do this and still have a narrow space feel big by having just a 3' high wall between the reception chairs and the hot seat area. The CA area is also designed perfectly and the success of this office proves it.

A re-configure of an existing office. Key is to make it better with the least construction and expense required. This doctor grew nearly 100 visits a week within a month of my new plan being implemented. At just $40 per visit that means a $200,000 per year collection increase with NO change in overhead. Imagine how that will change his life! Nobody is better at designing successful offices than we are.

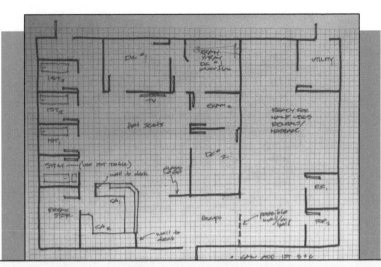

This doctor owned this building which already had two rest rooms and a utility room. Owner wanted a two DC office using the TR1000 IST tables. This office now sees over 350 visits a week and is only getting warmed up. Notice the need for two distinct CA work areas. To have CAs that like their job and stay for years, you must have a nice office that is designed well for them.

Look at this goofy shaped space. Odd spaces usually make for really cool designs. Notice how the CA can see every door like a good design allows. This place has a great open feel yet with privacy where desired. This is a really nice design where one DC could see 200 patients per day easily. Also in the top left see a room that could be rented to help offset rent and possibly get more patient referrals. An acupuncturist, hypnosis expert, or massage expert for example.

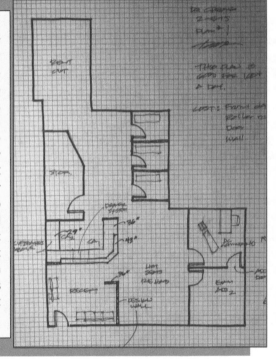

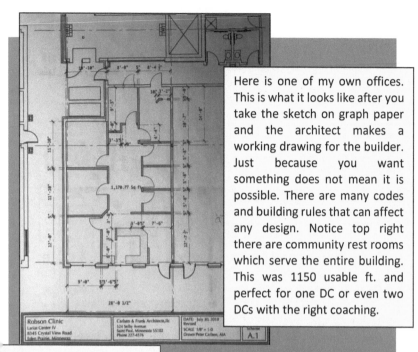

Here is one of my own offices. This is what it looks like after you take the sketch on graph paper and the architect makes a working drawing for the builder. Just because you want something does not mean it is possible. There are many codes and building rules that can affect any design. Notice top right there are community rest rooms which serve the entire building. This was 1150 usable ft. and perfect for one DC or even two DCs with the right coaching.

Here's the final product. There are 100 smart design elements here that would need to be explained. See the huge picture boards of me with patients giving massive validity. **Below:** Even though the space is small it feels big because of how far you can see when you walk in.

The colors, carpet, surfaces, door style, etc. are what I liked at the time. You may like a totally different look and that's great! When visiting offices always do more than just look at the decorating, ask what the rent is. Also, please don't be a mental peanut and copy people. Choose your own clinic name, colors, etc.

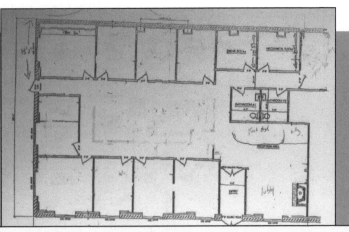

There are 3 DCs in the office above who want to see a lot more people. <u>Without changing any of the walls</u>, how are you going to re-purpose every area to make this happen? Remember, 3 DCs need 3 exam rooms, 3 X-ray machines, 3x as big a front desk, 3x as many chairs, 3x as much parking, 3x as many bathrooms, 3x as much therapy, and if all DCs want to reach their potential this office will need at least 4 - 6 CAs. You get the idea? Usually, no DC who brings in additional DCs ever really understands this. All the doctors then have their volume and collections choked without ever being able to identify why. They were very smart to call me. I am usually able to figure out the hairiest of situations. **Below:** What I recommended. This office collected $272,000 <u>more</u> their first year with us. Multiply that by 20 years left to practice = over $5,000,000 <u>more</u> collected! Was it worth the fee? What if they would have been too "smart" or too "cheap" to call me?

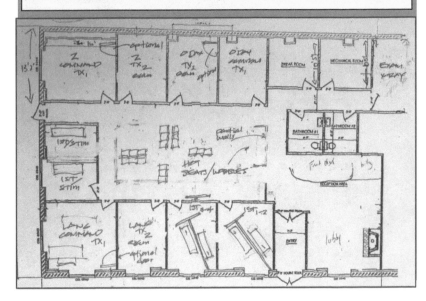

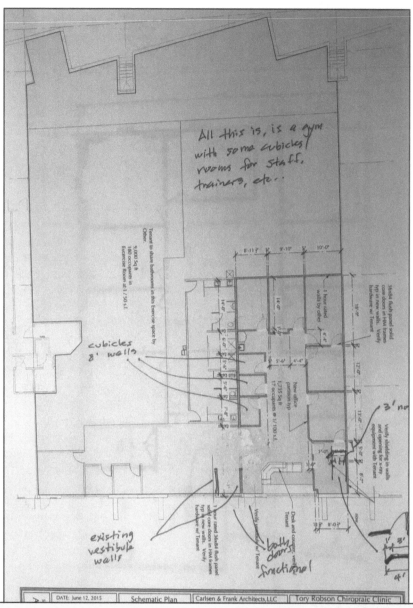

All this is, is a gym with some cubicles/ rooms for staff, trainers, etc.

cubicles 8' walls

existing vestibule walls

Tenant to share bathrooms in this Exercise space by Other.

9,000 Sq ft
180 occupants in Exercise Room at 1/50 L1

New office partition typ.
12,735 Sq ft
17 occupants @ 1/100 s.f.

Desk and counter verify w/ Tenant

Verify shielding in walls and opening for x-ray equipment with Tenant

Verify assembly w/ Tenant

both doors functional

1 hour rated walls by other

36x84 flush panel solid core doors in HM frames typ in new walls. Verify hardware w/ Tenant

1 hour rated 36x84 flush panel solid core doors in HM frames typ in new walls. Verify hardware w/ Tenant

DATE: June 12, 2015 | Schematic Plan | Carlsen & Frank Architects, LLC | Tory Robson Chiropraic Clinic

This is the office I'm in right now. I occupy 1800 ft. in the bottom right corner of this 11,200 ft. Fitness and Martial Arts center. This is not the place for a new DC to start. The gym flooring alone was $40,000 plus there was no air conditioning so it had to be installed via a crane on the roof for $15,000. It took me 20+ years of work and preparation to engineer this project successfully in such a way that everyone wins while I actually get paid to be here. For you though, just find a great space to get started!

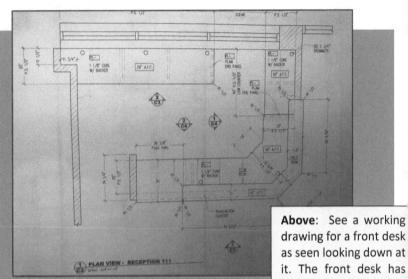

PLAN VIEW - RECEPTION 111

Invoice

November 27, 2015

Dr. Tory Robson
7116 Shady Oak Road
Eden Prairie, MN

Build out for Pro Spine chiropractic - Eden Prairie

Permit -	$8,397.28
Framing materials-steel studs-	$2,226.00
Electrical-	$17,885.60
Plumbing-	$800.00
Phone-	$2,417.14
Drywall, insulation & sound proofing-	$15,917.00
Door frames-	$1,974.31
Fire suppression-	$2,885.00
Suspended ceilings-	$2,892.00
HVAC-	$15,500.00
Lead-	$731.12
Counter Tops-	$5,057.00
Carpet in front of bathrooms, materials & labor-	$774.74
Lift rental-	$737.52
Haul off debris-	$254.60
Berryman Construction-Materials-	$2,532.79
Berryman Construction- labor @ 50.00 hr.	$7,050.00

Total-$88,032.10
10%-$8,803.21

Total- $96,835.31

Minus - Down Checks -$70,000.00

Total Due: $26,835.31

Thank you for your business,

Above: See a working drawing for a front desk as seen looking down at it. The front desk has many details. How tall, how wide, how thick? Corners with a nickel radius or soda can radius? 2" overhang or 4" overhang? What style of handles, where do the holes go for the computer cords, how many drawers, how deep are the drawers? Just call me on this when you are ready.

Left: This is a final invoice for a chiro office buildout. Look at every item. See the $15,000 for HVAC! You never know what it will really cost until it is all done. Some builders will give a low bid to get the job. Only to tell you later after they are half done that it will be more than expected.

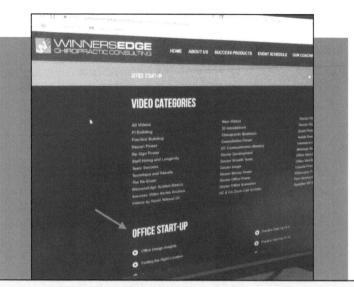

Above: See the Members Only Area of my website. There are 36 different categories containing over 500 instant videos on all elements of practice success. The **Office Start Up** category has been selected.

Below: A video showing me actually building one of my offices step by step from scratch. I have two videos like this. Many feel these videos alone are worth millions. It is devastating if you don't start right.

The flow of an office - Controls the volume of an office - Controls the money coming in to an office – Which affects everything in your life.

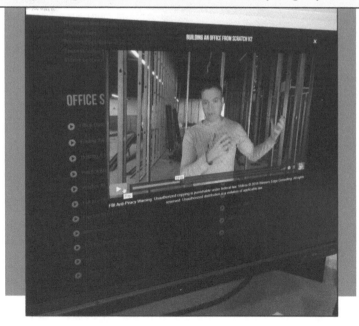

This is the office of a SERIOUS chiropractor. Look at all my educational ammo. This was 2003 - One of the first DCs to have a flat screen TV in the office! This office would easily seat 30 people and flow 1000.

Another high performance WINNERS**EDGE** office with the cool pendant lights, and a great CA area that can see everything. Notice how bright and incredible the sunlight looks coming in! No office I've had ever "felt" better than this one.

Every office must have as big a space as possible in the center. Not only for hot seats but also to do talks. *You gotta be able to pack 'em in!* Expect to get 10% of your weekly volume to attend any talks you do.

Current office with seating for 50+ easily. We also call this the WINNERS**EDGE** Chiro Training Center. Look at all these sharp powerhouse chiropractors learning the secrets to ultra-success so they can go back and break all their practice records!

Office Design Considerations:

- An office design is 100% a physics problem. Particles moving through a container or fluid dynamics through a container.

- The total amount of people who can flow through a space easily per unit of time is the MAIN concern, not paint colors.

- What you don't "see" in an office is what counts. When people visit my office, I say right away: *It is what you don't see that is impressive here.*

  Some offices look really cool but have a horrible design. Others look a tad plain but can flow a lot of people. Guess who wins? As is true with many things, function wins over appearance.

- A front desk where the CA faces into the office and can see all doors. How would you like to work in a place where you sit and have to stare at a front door or a wall all day, while all the action is going on somewhere behind you?

- If the ceiling can be left exposed I recommend it. This creates an open feel that is very nice.

- A DC command center for each doctor.

- Every CA needs a place to sit and work.

- An area in the middle as open as possible for people to sit.

- Just a few chairs up front for new patients to do paperwork. All current patients go sit in the hot seat area.

- The WINNERSEDGE way utilizes either a pure chiro office or the TR1000 IST flow model. The TR1000 is an intersegmental traction table made with my specifications. We also like the TR1. A Zenith adjusting table, also with my signature modifications.

- Step management is critical. How many steps does the doctor take to see a new patient, adjust people, or get to the front desk? Countless doctors lose $25,000 or more every year from walking so much because of a lousy design. Realize how true this is.

- We only get paid when we are actually with a patient. We never get paid for walking. Seconds are valuable when you add them up over a 41-year career.

- How many steps does a patient take to get adjusted? The fewer the better.

- We like the 4 colors of paint, carpet tiles, pendant lights, and wall sconces to make the place look great for very little cost.

- Where the referral board and patient picture boards will be mounted must be considered in the design.

- The DC command center directly next to the exam room with a trap door is the best. The DC command center and the exam/X-ray/second adjusting room allows the doctor to see as many people as time allows with very few steps. This allows great speed, but also with great privacy.

- The more open the adjusting is in an office, the less the doctor collects per visit. This has been proven for years.

- The WINNERSEDGE way is open adjusting speed with closed room privacy by utilizing a mirrored DC command center door. This way patients can see out of the room and notice others waiting, but those waiting cannot see in.

- One good computer up front and one for the doctor are all that are needed initially.

- A chiropractic office is very simple and does not need much technology. It can be done but it is not needed. As insurance companies pay less and become less important, offices can actually use LESS technology.

  My Travel Card note system is faster than any computer system and at practically no cost, no breakdown, no stress. Just because a computer can be used, never means it should be. Just like with surgeries, *just because a surgery can be done, doesn't always mean it should be done.*

- Where do you and your staff park? Where do you hang your jacket? Where do CAs put their jackets or purses?

- Always have a small fridge for icepacks.

- A break room is never needed. People eat too much and too often as it is.

- An office is like a race car, not a clunky station wagon. There is nothing unnecessary. Everything is designed for flow and speed.

- A standing front desk is a must. Walking in and seeing a CA sitting down in a chair is a disgrace. We care about our people enough that we get our tail up and ready for our patients. This is called "gravity defying" behavior in the body language training I do for doctors. It shows you are excited to see the person. This is one key to getting patients to want to come back forever.

- We have a specific hot seat chair we recommend with armrests. Chairs alone will cost over $2000. One of many items that you would not think of. Posters will cost another $1000.

- We recommend the black glass Referral and Welcome board as well as the absolute largest picture board you can fit. Load hundreds of pictures of you with patients, their new cars, their babies, all Thank You cards and anything else worth sharing.

- This shows VALIDITY. Doctors suffer when they have NO validity. No social proof that people think you are good = No patients. You need social proof!

  One HUGE picture board along with a jammed full Welcome and Referral board fixes this instantly. Even if there is nobody standing in your office you will still look busy and successful.

  People go where other people go because people go where other people go. This must be to YOU!

- When anyone walks in they should know it is a chiropractic office. It should reflect <u>all things chiropractic.</u>

Your office is simply the place where you go to deliver your art as efficiently and effectively as possible to as many people as possible. Nothing more.

Yes, we want it nice, but never forget it is a high-performance machine and must be designed and maintained as such.

I could write 1000 pages and show 100 examples of office design. All we can do in this book is give you a few smart ideas. Every office, location, state, doctor, and technique will all have their own exciting requirements.

Drill:

You find this perfect space in a great location. Draw a plan for your new office.
Notice the existing doors, windows and bathroom. Be sure to draw everything to
scale and add all equipment. 1 box=1 foot. What 4 colors you are going to use
and what color goes on which wall? Maybe quick do another drawing of how you
want your front desk. Then give it a clinic name, a URL, and create your new logo.

Looking at plans is easy. Making your own requires some serious thinking!

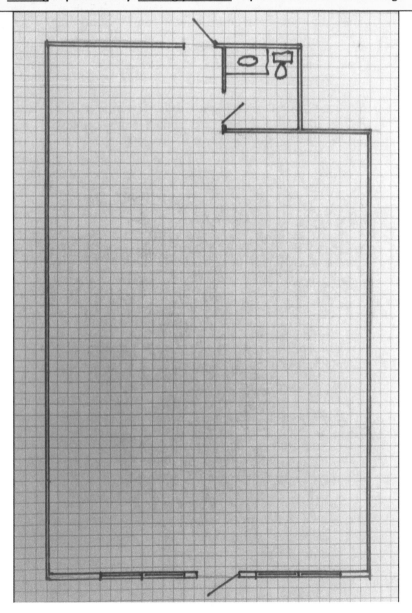

The main adjusting room door from the hot seat area. This is called a full light, birch, gold finish, solid core door with metal frame and a nickel plated locking lockset. I either order the doors mirrored or I have someone come in and mirror them. Either way works fine. Also notice the 18" decal. Decals placed properly can really add a nice professional touch.

Standing inside the main adjusting room. See the face paper squares, (I never use rolls on the table), a container for keys and phones, and a few hooks. Having this next to the door is handy. Also notice how you can see out the glass door. I almost never have the door fully shut when adjusting.

What do you notice here? See the corner shelves with Kleenex, table and hand spray, along with the Pure Ayre smell eliminator spray. See a bench I like for low back adjusting or for a family to sit on as I adjust them one at a time. Notice also every garbage can has a clean white liner in it at all times. The cool poster on the left looks especially good on this wall. ONLY chiropractic and social proof go on the walls of your office. No pictures of ducks, wedding photos, or anything else ever!

There is a lot more going on here than you think. It would take a few pages to explain. Notice the 4' wide wall when you enter. This protects the CAs and adds just enough additional privacy plus keeps people from being able to see behind the front desk. It blocks the cold air in the winter, provides the perfect place for the coat hooks, provides an optimal place to have a desk, and cupboards attached to the other side of it make space for a perfect CA workstation. Also observe the alarm controller is here.

What all do you notice here? Clinic logo pens only, a chiropractic magazine, and a jammed full Referral and Welcome board on a wall specifically designed for it. Notice the 4 light switches smartly placed on this wall and not by the front door. This way we have control over all light at all times. Also with brushed nickel to match the door handles and outlets. The double bank drawer system I always recommend and the ideal place for the fridge that fits perfectly since the front desk is designed at the correct height of 36". Is it clean? Of course it is! The best offices are always clean with no clutter anywhere.

Left: The walkway to go behind the front desk. 36" wide minimum. A perfect place for team coat hooks, the Heat/AC controller, and the knob for the ceiling fan. The ceiling is 16' high so a fan is smart to have. In the winter the heat rises and this blows it back down very nicely. Notice how great the lighting is in all pictures. Your office must be bright, healthy, and ALIVE!

Right: What do you see in this exam/X-ray room picture? Notice the large carpet tiles. The bench on the right is by far the best place for a patient to sit for a consult. Four people can fit on one while you examine one at a time. The Gonstead chair with the back flipped down. I can examine the spine while facing a mirror so the patients can see my facial expressions as I talk. The exam is CRITICAL education time. See the digital X-ray. Notice the patient goes from the bench where we talk, to the chair where I examine, to then standing where we do X-rays. All patients are trained to know what happens where. I also am trained to be in the correct mindset every time I see a patient in a particular spot in the office, especially the adjusting room. Consults are done on the bench, exams in the chair, and adjusting in the adjusting room!

Everything must have a reason to be there. The office is a race car. A race car only has what is required for high performance.

Imagine your new office was a car. Do you want a slow wagon, a clunky truck with all sorts of gadgets stuck to it, a cheap little burner with no power, or a high-performance machine? *How about **YOU**. Are you a slow outdated wagon? Are **YOU** clunky truck, are **YOU** trying to "cheap" your way through life, or are **YOU** a high performance machine?*

MODULE 8   *Time to Equip the Place and Get Ready*

Once the buildout is complete and the space is ready to occupy, it is now time to fill it. Here is a basic list of things you will need. Think of it in terms of what is needed for <u>each room</u> when making your list.

<u>The very first thing</u> to get, that nobody ever thinks of, is a tool box loaded with the right tools. You have no idea how often you will need this. You can thank me in advance for this bit of great advice.

Toolbox:

- Screwdrivers, a level, various sizes of small nails and drywall screws, pliers, cutters, drywall anchors, hanging hooks for posters, masking tape, drywall dent filler, putty knife, magic eraser, a couple small paintbrushes to touch up wall dings (keep a can of each color paint and make sure the cans have the paint code on them!) a good multi-tool kit with Allen wrenches, a cordless drill, drill bits, box cutter, and of course a hammer.

Office Furniture:

- Reception and hot seat chairs, always with armrests.
- Coat hooks and cork boards for picture wall.

Doctor Command Center:

- Desk and the file cabinet that fits underneath it. We have a specific desk and file cabinet we recommend that is a proven winner.
- Diplomas framed and hung perfectly.
- Wall mounted bookshelf.
- Smart chiropractic posters.
- White board.
- Computer, printer, and phone.
- Good "German" spine with foam discs.
- Exercise handouts.
- Spray table cleaner.
- Pure Ayre spray to get smells off hands and tables. Also <u>sugar scrub</u> by Qtica on *Amazon*. This is the ONLY thing that will get perfume or cologne off your hands. You will thank me for this tip. These are a life saver!

- Hanging file folders for: Continuing Ed, Malpractice Ins, the EIN SS4 form, copies of State License, all banking, everything.

Exam Room:
- Exam table. I prefer a <u>fabric covered</u> Gonstead bench. It is perfect for people to sit on for consultations plus it can seat 4 people.
- Cervical chair with the back in the down position for exams.
- Mirror placed on the wall in front of the patient being examined.
- Exam tools.
- Bilateral weight scales.
- Dynamometer.
- Gown holder, gowns and gown hamper.
- X-ray unit and all its equipment including battery backup.
- Possibly an EMG if a doctor desires it to use in place of X-ray.
- I see no need for both X-ray and EMG.

CA, Reception, and Hot Seat Area:
- Drafting stool with back removed for CA#1.
- Garbage cans and bags to line them.
- 2 or 4-line phones as needed.
- Business card holders and pen holders.
- At least 2000 business cards and 500 for each staff member.
- Small cash box or drawer organizer to hold cash and change.
- 1000 letterhead and envelopes.
- Extra ream of <u>blank letterhead paper</u> for multi-page documents.
- Computers.
- Printers. Always get the same brand with the same print cartridge. Smart to have at least one good color printer in the office.
- Fax machine/printer. No need to spend much here and certainly never rent one from any equipment supply/copier company. These people will find you once you open and sound fairly convincing. I have used a $299 HP Fax Copier for 8 years.
- A case of copy paper.
- Any other file cabinets, shelves, storage systems needed.
- Plants - I never recommend plants in a chiro office.
- Posters - Always framed and hung perfectly.
- White board to have chiropractic fun fact or quote for patients.

- All office supplies including a lot of hanging file folders, staplers, paper clips, tape, pen holders, pens, pencils, Sharpies, colored pens, highlighters, Post-it notes, white board pens, microfiber towels, good scissors and a calculator for every desk are a must.
- At least 6 clipboards. Put your clinic decal on the back of them.
- Small fridge for icepacks. Our office designs have a specific place for the fridge to fit perfectly.
- Icepacks with your clinic name on them. We like *accurategelpacks.com* for giveaway ice packs.
- Mirrors 36 x 48 for all IST rooms.
- 24 x 36 black glass dry erase for Referral and Welcome board.

Forms and Paperwork to Have:
- Intake paperwork including the Paying for Your Care sheet.
- ABNs for Medicare.
- Work Comp and PI paperwork.
- Pediatric paperwork.
- Exam Forms and Care Plan sheets.
- HIPAA handout.
- Medicare brochure from *customchirosolutions.com.*
- Doctor pads to write Doctors notes when needed.
- Records request forms.
- Plain, regular, and 9 x 12 envelopes.
- Welcome cards and Thank You cards.
- Rolls of regular and post card stamps.

Additional Supplies:
- Pledge, carpet cleaner like *Resolve*, white board cleaner, *Goo Gone*, white rags, alcohol, Super Glue.
- Hand soap and paper towel holder.
- Bathroom supplies if necessary.
- Quantity packs of AA and AAA batteries.
- Various sizes of Band Aids. Trust me you will need them.
- A couple candles to make sure the office always smells nice.
- Good vacuum cleaner.
- Clinic logo decals in 10" and 18" length. Get 10 of each.

Music in Office:

- We recommend two SONOS speakers for music. Never have speakers in any treating area or in the CA area. Music is only in the reception and hot seat area to muffle conversations, fill with some sound, and add a little life.

Never play music with an agenda. You may love Country, Hip Hop, Sports Talk Radio or be a devout Christian but leave that for your car and home. Your office is for your patients, not you.

Be smart and play neutral, universally accepted music. Best is music with no words. You can't imagine how many doctors think their office is an extension of their home. This is amateur level, self-centered, and repels a lot of patients. Which also means it repels money.

Once you have no student loans and at least $1 million saved then you can wear flip flops and play whatever you want in your office.

A properly dressed doctor and another happy patient who loves coming in for her regular adjustments. See the perfectly level wall pieces. Be sure to never have any power cords visible anywhere. Cord management is yet another detail that makes an office top notch.

The above elements will get you pretty close to ready. All this is done for one reason and one reason only, so you can have a beautifully running office that will attract and serve thousands of patients. It is not all about the race car. It is about racing the race car!

I see doctors hung up on getting the office ready and forget that it is just a formality to get to the REAL project which is taking care of people!

The entire time you are building and preparing an office, your mind is on how you are going to get 100 new patients in there as fast as you can.

How can I get 100 new patients in here as fast as possible?

Above: Notice the incredible picture board and diplomas. Anyone who walks in here will be impressed. It is FREE to impress people. Bright, clean, organized. **Left**: Notice the trap door to the X-ray room. This doctor down in Florida can do it all from his DC command center!

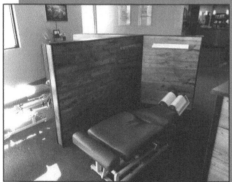

This dynamic two female team loves their new semi open adjusting design. Notice the CA desk and cool pendant lights in the distance. See how smart it is for the doctor and CAs to instantly be able to communicate. With their new WE design they are now a 400 visit a week team.

Great colors, open feel, lots of room to flow patients. This doctor collected $200,000 <u>more</u> his first year with WE. That was <u>before</u> he settled into his incredible WE designed office. He's now broken all his practice records many times over.

CA is able to see IST and DC command center door. This doctor is ready for more picture boards! From the doorway if the DC tells a patient to come back Monday, the CA automatically hears it. This is a critical ability you want to have in your office.

Notice from the front door you can see 'into' the office. This is how we make a small space feel bigger and more welcoming. Angles are also important. It is amazing how one angled wall will open up the flow of an office.

The awesome TR1000.

Above: This doctor could not figure out why nobody wanted to come see him.

Compare this disaster to the picture to the left of it. A perfect DC command center with trap door to the X-ray and nice light. What a great place to work.

If you want to be ultra-successful, your primary success team will be YOU, your practice success expert consultant like ME, and your ACCOUNTANT. You will occasionally need an attorney or other experts. Notice nowhere in here were your parents, husband, wife, boyfriend or girlfriend mentioned. They can all be involved and have an opinion, but expert and experienced advice is what we base our decisions on.

I have now had over 50,000 calls with chiropractors everywhere for every issue you can imagine and 1000 that you can't. In practically 100% of cases where I hear a DC say: *Hold on, my husband or wife wants to be on the call with us* I know right then we might have a problem.

Successful doctors and business owners run their own show. They evaluate, make decisions, then tell those around them what they did, if it even gets talked about at all. The successful doctor is what is called a benevolent dictator. This means they are a nice, smart, capable person who with self-direction runs the show without excuse or apology to anyone. They operate in such a way that others respect and trust them.

They don't ask whoever is around them what to do. They ask their coach and accountant before they do, buy, add, change, or eliminate anything. Then they simply do it and let others see the prosperous fruit of their smart thoughts and actions.

Some doctors are weak. Some doctors screw things up so much that it's no wonder their spouses are trying to tell them what to do. We see cases where if the spouse were the doctor the office would be busier.

Are you a person who can make good decisions?

The real winner never needs to ask or get permission from anyone in their household for decisions that relate to their business. Do you ask your patients what you should do in your home life? No. So why ask those at home what you should do in your business? Who made them experts anyway?

I bring this up because doctors get out of school and often start looking to the wrong people for advice. We have been taught our entire life that parents, teachers, professors, and bosses direct our big decisions.

We then graduate and now for the first time in our lives we are in total control. People tend to go back to their past programing and start saying things like: *What should I do?* or ask: *What would you do?* to literally anyone around whether they have relevant expertise or not.

Think of any awesome company you can imagine: Chipotle, Panera Bread, Oakley, Apple, US Bank. Do you think the CEO of any of these companies has to ask their spouse before they make any corporate decisions? Heck no! Big company or small company makes no difference. The independent thinking success principle is exactly the same.

Some doctors let their spouse, kids, CAs and even patients tell them what to do, and worse yet, even push them around. I hate to see it!

To be successful in business we trust only those who are proven experts in the exact thing we are trying to do.

We might talk with those close to us to get ideas and discuss things, but we sure as the sun is hot don't answer to them or take their advice over the advice of those who are experts.

Here at **WINNERSEDGE** I teach independence and self-reliance. We want to carefully evaluate any ideas and just before we are ready to make a decision ask the coach or accountant to review it. Then it is time for you to confidently make the decision never look back.

Today there are a lot of people who like to talk a lot. They want to be bossy, act smart, and tell others what to do <u>without</u> first being the real thing themselves. They are not follow-worthy. Do not get caught listening to them, and more importantly, never be like that yourself.

Read, study, work hard, make smart decisions, be prudent, show up early, stay late, always be on time, prepare more than anyone else, see the future more clearly, train harder, look sharper, be better with money, do what you say, finish what you start, and impress people. You will then be trusted. People will believe in you and want to follow you!

You be the Coach:

A doctor asks you: *How can I get more referrals?*

Your answer?

My answer: *Well doctor, <u>are you making referrals</u>? You have to GIVE more referrals first! You have to plant seeds first to get any harvest! Even if you just think of giving referrals it will work. A <u>get</u> mindset gets little. A GIVE mindset brings the return! Plus, you might want to make sure your service is good enough to make people talk about you!*

The Success Team of the *Ultra-Successful* DC

You: Those who want to be the best in their profession want to learn all they can about it, allowing them to be assertive and sure footed.

Your Practice Success Consultant: For experience, procedures, systems, motivation, events, resources, personal and team development.

Being in a group is essential as every doctor NEEDS these three:

1. Motivation from those better and <u>more successful than you.</u>

2. To consistently interact and grow with those at your <u>same level.</u>

3. To share and help those <u>not as advanced</u> as you.

Our group provides all this. It makes practice and life much more fun. Consulting fees are 100% tax deductible. Even the government thinks you should have a consultant!

Your Accountant: We always have payroll, accounting, W2s, W4s, 941s, tax returns, and questions about expenses, purchases, hiring, firing, tax strategy, and planning. This keeps the successful doctor in contact with the accountant. The more successful you become the more this is true.

A doctor who never talks to their accountant is probably not a very successful doctor. My accountant is at every seminar I teach as a resource for me and my clients. He handles chiropractors exclusively and his dad did for 30 years before him. He is an incredible asset!

Our online video series for our clients called: ***The Chiro Business and Accounting Bootcamp*** is two hours on all the vital elements of practice business and accounting. Including all the things a chiropractor can write-off as a business expense, and just as importantly, all the things a chiropractor cannot write-off, but "thinks" they can.

Question: Which of the following can you pay from your business checking account? See how you need to ask an accountant!

❑ Gas to get to and from work.

❑ Lunch at work.

❑ Taking an attorney out for lunch.

❑ Golf with other DCs.

❑ A personal cell phone that patients call occasionally.

- ❏ Your gym membership.
- ❏ Student loan payments.
- ❏ Your car insurance.
- ❏ Your disability policy.
- ❏ Clothes to wear at work.
- ❏ T-shirts with your logo on them.
- ❏ CA outfits.
- ❏ All seminar airline, hotel, and food expenses.
- ❏ A new piece of luggage to use for seminars.
- ❏ Cash from the clinic account to give as a bonus to a CA.
- ❏ Success books to read from *Amazon*.
- ❏ A new suit just to wear to chiropractic seminars.
- ❏ A fluoride removal water filter *(pure-earth.com)*.
- ❏ Tools that you will keep at work for when needed.
- ❏ A new computer to have at home.

Attorneys: You will need an attorney for any contracts, hiring or firing issues, and real estate concerns. You will need personal injury and workers comp attorneys as required for patient cases.

MRI Center: Call, get a tour, and have referral pads. A busy office will certainly have patients that need MRIs from time to time.

MD, Ortho, or Neurologist: Chiropractic appreciative MDs are everywhere and are super valuable. Whenever you are not sure about anything, confidently refer them to a local medical contact you have.

Physical Therapist: You are a great chiropractor, but if a person can benefit from some PT feel free to send them there. They will often make referrals back as they know you are much better with adjusting spines.

Financial Advisor: Rarely needed until debt is gone and you are ready to invest. At **WINNERSEDGE,** we want to keep money flow as simple as possible. We have many recommendations in this area.

Insurance Agent: Another person you will deal with a lot. Try to have everything at the same place. I currently have all my insurance, except for my malpractice, with one local agent. I get major multi policy discounts. To give you an idea, I have 14 different policies with my agent.

Banker: Normally only possible in smaller towns where the bank manager is not replaced every 6 months. If you can get on a first name basis with a local banker this can be beneficial.

Other experts: An IT expert for computer, networking and internet issues. Electricians, plumbers, carpet cleaners and anyone who is an expert with what you need. Make friends with everyone who helped build your office. You will need them again sometime!

Whenever you need anything you want to know who to call. Save business cards and names of anyone you feel might be valuable sometime in the future. What you know is important, but your power will come from <u>knowing someone for everything.</u> Remember, a good friend is a person who helps their friends and acquaintances make more money. Refer to these people as often as you can!

It really isn't that hard to be the best, it is simply a matter of outworking your opposition. But most people don't know to push themselves to their true potential.
- Dan Gable
Olympic Gold medalist. Top 100 Olympians of all time, and one of the most dominant coaches in NCAA history. His teams won the Big 10 Conference Championship <u>all</u> 21 years he coached. Incredible.

Dan Gable is known for being one of the hardest working wrestlers and athletes who ever lived. Nearly all training protocols to push yourself beyond your limits can be credited to him. He needed hip replacements at 49 because he wore them out from training so hard. In college he would run with ankle weights between class, and twist rope with his hands while in class. He did not want to miss a minute of opportunity to make himself better.

IF YOU'RE IN YOUR COMFORT ZONE THEN YOU'RE STILL WARMING UP

Clinic and CA #1 Schedule for a New Office

38-40 CA Hours

	MON	TUE	WED	THU	FRI
7:30					
8:00					
8:30	CA Clean	Team Mtg	CA Clean	CA Clean	CA Clean
9:00	Huddle	Huddle	Huddle	Huddle	Huddle
9:30	Adjust	Adjust CA Billing	Adjust	Adjust	Adjust
10:00					
10:30					
11:00					
11:30					
12:00	Wrap-up	Wrap-up	Wrap -up	Wrap-up	Wrap-up
12:30					
1:00					
1:30					
2:00					
2:30	Huddle	Huddle	Huddle	Huddle	Huddle
3:00	Adjust	Adjust	Adjust	Adjust	Adjust
3:30					
4:00					
4:30					
5:00					
5:30					
6:00	Huddle	Huddle	Huddle	Huddle	Huddle
6:30					

- You cannot be there early morning, around lunch, <u>and</u> in the afternoon all in one day without burning out over time.

- You must choose two of the three. The clear choice is lunch and afternoon as the span of the day is debilitating if you choose mornings and afternoons.

- I also recommend seeing patients from 9-10 Saturday morning.

After 100 visits/wk is maintained upgrade to this:
Hours: 40 CA #1 + 20 CA #2

	MON	TUE	WED	THU	FRI
7:30					
8:00					
8:30	CA Clean	Team Mtg	CA Clean	CA Clean	CA Clean
9:00	Huddle	Huddle	Huddle	Huddle	Huddle
9:30	Adjust	Adjust CA Billing	Adjust	Adjust	Adjust
10:00					
10:30					
11:00					
11:30					
12:00	Wrap-up	Wrap-up	Wrap -up	Wrap-up	Wrap-up
12:30					
1:00					
1:30					
2:00					
2:30	Huddle	Huddle	Huddle	Huddle	
3:00	Adjust	Adjust	Adjust	Adjust	
3:30					
4:00					
4:30					
5:00					
5:30					
6:00	Huddle	Huddle	Huddle	Huddle	
6:30					

- After 100+ visits per week is established, IF and only if the <u>practice is profitable</u> and solid, then and <u>only</u> then can a DC remove Friday afternoon from the clinic schedule. Having Friday afternoon 'off' is the reward for sustaining 100+ visits per week!

- Consider an afternoon CA at 30+ visits a day and a second full time CA at 50+ visits a day depending on therapy requirements if any.

After 200 visits/wk is maintained upgrade to this:

Hours: 36 CA #1 + 36 CA #2

	MON	TUE	WED	THU	FRI
7:30					
8:00					
8:30	CA Clean	CA Clean	CA Clean	CA Clean	CA Clean
9:00	Huddle	Team Mtg	Huddle	Huddle	Huddle
9:30	Adjust	Billing	Adjust	Adjust	Adjust
10:00		All Paperwork			
10:30		Done			
11:00		**No**			
11:30		**Patients**			
12:00	Huddle		Huddle	Huddle	Huddle
12:30					
1:00					
1:30					
2:00					
2:30	Huddle	Huddle	Huddle	Huddle	
3:00	Adjust	Adjust	Adjust	Adjust	
3:30					
4:00					
4:30					
5:00					
5:30					
6:00	Huddle	Huddle	Huddle	Huddle	
6:30					

- Notice individual staff hours decrease as you get busier also!
- Now have 2 cross-trained CAs who can do <u>everything</u>.
- The WE **Rapid Fire** and **Vortex Savings** should be established.
- The doctor's level of fitness must be elevated.

After 300 visits/wk is maintained then upgrade to this:

Hours: 34 CA #1 + 34 CA #2 + 20 CA #3 Hours

	MON	TUE	WED	THU	FRI
7:30					
8:00					
8:30	CA Clean	CA Clean	CA Clean	CA Clean	
9:00	Huddle	Team Mtg	Huddle	Huddle	Dr. and CA
9:30	Adjust	Billing	Adjust	Adjust	Finish
10:00		All			Weekly
		Paperwork			Paperwork
10:30		Done			**No Patients**
		No			
11:00		**Patients**			
11:30					
12:00	Huddle		Huddle	Huddle	
12:30					
1:00					
1:30					
2:00					
2:30	Huddle	Huddle	Huddle	Huddle	
3:00	Adjust	Adjust	Adjust	Adjust	
3:30					
4:00					
4:30					
5:00					
5:30					
6:00	Huddle	Huddle	Huddle	Huddle	
6:30					

- Our recommended DC hours, CA hours and clinic open times are a time tested and proven winner for longevity.

- This schedule allows for volume plus doctor and staff off-time.

- Possibly add an additional afternoon CA if needed.

- A qualified high school student can make a great extra CA.

- The right schedule allows the entire clinic team to practice gracefully for years - avoiding burnout.

- It makes it easy to attend seminars and trainings for even more advancement.

- Goal is to get to this level as **fast** as possible. Shoot for 90 days.

- The ultimate schedule is three or four half-days per week.

- Remember, your <u>Treatment Time</u> controls your volume.

- Declutter, stay organized, stay fresh = Lasting success.

- Doctor should be in a "Master Mind" group with other success minded people. Being in our group accomplishes this perfectly.

- Doctor should attend seminars, read, and listen to audios.

- Do all tasks perfectly each day. Leave your desk clean. CAs too!

<u>The Pre-Shift Huddle:</u> *These are CRITICAL! Never miss a huddle!*

- Go over <u>every single name</u> in the book and who to call.

- Mark if they need anything like a financial fix, special attention, a referral packet, or asked if you can come in to speak. Note anything that is care, payment arrangement, or parlay related.

- Awareness of opportunities during the huddle is what builds a big referral practice. This happens because the <u>doctor and team are paying attention to the people in front of them</u> vs. always worrying about trying to "get more new ones."

<u>The Post-Shift Huddle:</u>

- Quickly assesses how well the shift went, plus any needs or planning thoughts for the next shift. Always think growth.

<u>The Weekly Team Meeting:</u>

- 30 minutes once a week. It is <u>the most important 30 minutes of the week</u>! Follow the WINNERS**EDGE** Team Meeting Agenda. It assures all that needs to be done is getting done. Plus, it keeps everyone focused on the clinic goals and <u>on the patients</u>. Think about your patients and they will think about and call you!

We have had our entire lives planned out for us by schools, parents, teachers, and bosses. Then, the day we graduate for good, we suddenly must be able to plan our own days, weeks, months, years, and life! This handy weekly schedule we use is perfect for writing in your plan for a great week.

Being able to read these schedules is not important, simply knowing that they exist is enough for now.

This is how full a week looks for a doctor who wants to see 100+ patients per day. 6am to 11pm is accounted for. Weekends are perfect practice building time. Family is important. This means it is your job FIRST to create an income to support yourself and any family you have. You will hear this often: *If you love your family you will make money to support them in a wonderful way.*

WINNERSEDGE CHIROPRACTIC CONSULTING — TEAM MEETING Agenda

1. Our **PURPOSE** is to attract, love, and treat _____ + patients and _____ PI patients per week towards optimal health with natural chiropractic and massage!

2. **Key Elements**: ↑ NP ↑ Visits ↑ Retention ↑ Collections ↑ Referrals!

3. **Goals**: _____ + per week _____ PI vis week Collect $ ___ k+ per mo _____ new PIs per month
   _____ +PI messages a wk

   - We are now happy and thankful to attract all required to reach these goals. WGTAC
   - We love and are now attracting referrals from new patients, past patients, lawyers, friends, family, restaurants, clubs, meetings, and beyond!
   - Goal for all patients to refer at least one person in for care.
   - Attract and start at least 2+ new PI's every week.
   - All paperwork and insurance complete for every patient.
   - Solid financial plans and appointment making for all patients.

4. WINS _____

5. Upcoming Events: Screenings Talks Seminars Holidays: _____

6. Stats _____

7. NP Log _____

8. Recent Patient Status and Records _____

9. Recall List _____

10. PI list Billing - Ins - Pt Bills _____

11. Parlay _____

12. Atty Cards _____

13. Appointments every time or on recall _____

14. Read Referral Triggers _____

15. Cards/Thank You's _____

The amazing WINNERSEDGE 30-minute Team Meeting Agenda. ALL top offices have a weekly team meeting and never miss. This is what keeps a practice running great. It is <u>the most important 30 minutes of the week</u>.

All my clients get the Microsoft Word files and access to training videos for all these documents and many more. Having these makes you ready to grow immediately.

We offer, or you might say, we sell the following services. The *5 Plays* as we call them. Yes, we also may offer X-rays, Re-exams, and other services, but for now observe the following key procedures.

Consultation: You sit with the patient and understand why they are there and what they are hoping for. You gather <u>subjective</u> findings. *Your goal is for them to feel you are an expert who is capable of helping them.*

Exam: You examine the patient and gather <u>objective</u> findings. Primarily spasm, fixation, and tenderness. *Goal here is for the patient to know that you have found IT, and that you know exactly where IT is, and that you have preliminary confidence on being able to help them with IT.*

Report of Findings: You go over the **P**roblem, the **P**lan, and the **P**ayment arrangement. The **3 P's** as we call them. *Your goal here is to get them to start an initial plan of care with confidence in you and in chiropractic.*

Office Visits: You want to package your art and skill into the tightest and most concentrated unit of time. You want to get the best results. You want to make people want to come see you forever as their chiropractor. You do this by having a great office visit that is time conscious.

Re-Sign: Procedure where you skillfully guide the patient to stay under care in a wellness Plan. Ideally with their entire family. Getting a patient to stay under care with you starts the moment they walk in as a new patient.

<u>Key CPT codes to know.   CPT = Current Procedural Terminology</u>

99203 The most commonly used exam service/code. Common fee range of $90 to $175. (I just paid $335 for this at an ortho office for my shoulder. The PA was in the room maybe 7 minutes.)

98940 Spinal adjustment to 1 or 2 regions of the spine. Common fee range is $40 to $70.

98941 Spinal adjustment to 3 or 4 regions of the spine. Common fee range is $50 to $80.

99212-25 Brief Re-exam code with the -25 modifier meaning the patient was also adjusted the same day but that the exam was a separate and distinct service from the spinal adjustment.

99213-25 Re-exam also with -25 modifier. If they receive only an exam that day with no adjusting, then the code would be 99212 or 99213 with no modifier.

X-ray and Therapy codes:

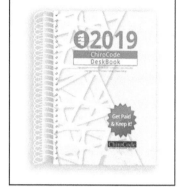

Refer to the *Chiro Code Desk Book.* Every DC should have one. It defines all codes, procedures, and pricing values for all services.

Let me ask you a question: *How much do you, yes YOU reading this right now, currently pay to see the chiropractor?* Nothing right? You probably never have to pay anything to get adjusted. Friends adjust you for free. If you visit a chiropractic office they usually adjust you for free.

Next question: *How much do you believe an adjustment is worth?* You pay zero. Let me clue you in, you have been programmed to think it is worth zero. Yet the day you graduate you will need to suddenly, both consciously and subconsciously, have a correct value for the very thing you are about to sell.

The truth I just described here is THE biggest reason why so many doctors have a hard time charging a patient the correct amount. Because of this, doctors can be nervous and weak when it is time tell a patient their balance and payment options. There is a deep-rooted value problem that every chiropractor needs to fix.

I believe many adjustments are actually worth millions because of how much impact they have on a person's life. I have concluded in my mind that anytime I adjust any person it is worth $100. I may have them pay something different, but in my mind adjustments are priceless and no fee can cover it. A typical office visit and adjustment is worth at least $100.

People "get to pay." Paying their bill is actually part of their healing. Once a patient pays, they then *expect* something. What they expect are

RESULTS. We want them to expect this. This is one reason why patients who prepay tend to do better than people who pay little out of pocket. Those that pay the least seem to complain the most.

We use very smart wording to lay out patient care plans. This is required to explain payment options in such a way that the patient wants to start care. This is a critical part of the basic training every doctor needs.

If you can't get cash patients to sign up for care and pay you, then it is going to be a long road. The WE systems make signing up patients quite easy. They may be the best systems in the profession today.

The ultimate in skill is to have a family prepay cash for their entire care plan, then prepay every year for wellness care.

I can't tell you what your fees or care plans should be, I can only guide you. We basically only do 5 things with 5 different types of people. It is pretty straightforward but being a master at them will require work.

The incredible Care Plan sheet. It is THE piece of paper that defines what a patient gets plus how much and when they pay.

This one sheet is literally worth millions. Using the wrong form, or no form is a disaster. You must have the right forms in place for everything!

We Deliver Our Services to These 5 People:

Cash Patients: No insurance involved whatsoever. Cash, check, credit or debit card.

Insurance Patients: Patient has some health insurance to file that may or may not pay anything. Plan to become an expert with this.

Medicare: Person has the red white and blue Medicare card with Part B benefits. Plan to become an expert at this.

Personal Injury: Normally this is someone who has been injured in an auto crash either as a driver, passenger, or pedestrian. Can also be a slip and fall, an injury boating, snowmobiling, jet skiing, or on a motorcycle. Essentially any injury where there may be insurance in place to pay for it. There must be an incident that causes an injury. Being hurt is not the same as being injured. An injury has objective findings. Every state has different laws regarding these claims. Plan right now to become an expert with patients who have been injured!

Work Injury: Injury in a work setting where there is a Workers Compensation policy in place to cover the cost of care. Every state has different rules here. Plan to become an expert at this. The best way to learn is by having cases.

The next best thing is to have lunches with PI and Work Comp attorneys. Get them talking about how cases and insurance companies work.

You can see that the intricacies of Medicare, a motorcycle crash, or a work injury can appear complicated and daunting. With a good consultant and all the resources in your consulting group, any questions you may have are <u>instantly answered</u> so you can gain expertise quickly.

Meanwhile, your goal is to have perfectly memorized procedures and scripting, especially the Report of Findings. We have the step by step procedures and precise scripting for practically every patient scenario.

The best way to explain things has already been figured out. I recommend you use what is proven to work and not try to wing it.

Each item below has its own training required that is beyond what we can do here. We have all our procedural and scripting details in print plus audio and video form for our clients.

<u>Procedures to MASTER:</u>

- New patient phone call using the NP Call Log pad.
- Day 1 new patient procedure by CA when the new patient arrives.
- Doctor - patient hand-off by CA and doctor greeting of the patient.
- **Consultation** scripting is vital.
- **Exam** flow and power. Must strip the authority from the patient.
- **X-ray** or **EMG** procedure. This is a great time to educate.
- Day 2 **Report** of Findings. The **3 P's**.
    - Report of **Problem** scripting.
    - Report of **Plan** with scripting using the incredible WINNERSEDGE report diagram. We draw a diagram!
    - Report of **Payment** arrangement using the Care Plan sheet.

- The ideal **Office visit** must be defined. Know what a perfect office visit is. Then you can have thousands of them!

- The **Re-exam** process and scripting as needed based on the three different responses of same, better, or worse.

- The **Re-sign** process to get people to want to enjoy ongoing wellness care in your office.

Example:

What room does the patient go in, where exactly do they sit, how and when does the doctor come in, how is the greeting performed, with what wording, what type of handshake does the doctor use, where does the doctor sit, what is on the walls behind the doctor that the patient sees as the consult occurs, where does the patient move for the exam, what is the exam procedure, what language is used?

We must be very good with our procedures. In a more descriptive sense I will explain what we are actually selling. Promoting, offering, call it whatever you like. I like selling because that is exactly what it is. I love selling and I especially love selling chiropractic because it is so amazing.

All our procedures are designed to be what you would want yourself. If you were out of state and went to a chiropractor, what would you want to have happen yourself? Describe the ideal experience step by step. Is this what you deliver to others right now?

If you have a loved one in another state go to a chiropractor, what do you want to see occur for them? Is this what you sell in your office?

Do you offer the very thing that you want yourself?

What I am saying here is incredibly profound! Most DCs do not do what they would like themselves. Then they wonder why they are not seeing as many patients and collecting as much money as they would like.

Doctors want to get right in, but in their own office they make people wait because they are unscripted and slow. They want the doctor they see to just tell them straight what the deal is, but with their own patients they are long winded and never really lay it out clearly.

They want their own billing and payment arrangements clearly understood, yet with their patients they are sloppy with billing and payment arrangements. They want a doctor who is in great physical condition and looks sharp, yet they are a little lumpy, weak, and not dressed that well themselves.

You want to <u>be in alignment</u>. What you THINK, what you SAY and what you DO must all be congruent. Many doctors *think* one thing, *tell* patients another thing, then go and *do* something totally different.

What I Would Want If I Was A New Patient:

1. I want to walk right in and see an impeccably clean, bright, alive office that smells nice with light music in the background. I see a loaded referral board showing others trust them and a few people with smiles on their faces waiting or checking out.

2. I want a healthy looking, happy CA to be standing as she smiles at me and says: *Hey you must be Tory, I'm Sherri, I just have a couple sheets here for you to do. Make sure you complete all areas and sign it, then just bring it back up when you are done and we'll get you right back with Dr. Awesome!*

3. I want to bring my clipboard up and hear her say: *Great, it will be just a second.* Then literally seconds later hear her say: *Tory c'mon back, have a seat here, he'll be right in. Dr. Awesome is looking forward to meeting you!*

   She puts me in a clean exam room with chiropractic posters on the walls. Literally one minute later the doctor opens the door.

4. The doctor assertively bolts in, clipboard in left hand, right hand extended to shake hands. Looking athletic, well read, well trained, capable, and very sharp with a great handshake he says: *Tory it is great to meet you, call me Dr. Awesome.*

4. The doctor then gets right to the point: *I see your paper work here but let me still ask, what is the main thing bothering you the most that you want me to help you with Tory?*

   My low back.

   Show me.

   It is right here.

Yep, I know just what this is like. I see about 20 of these every day. Take your shirt off and let's take a careful look at it.

5. Doctor finds the exact spot and says: *That's it right there isn't it?*

   Yes.

   He says: *We gotta' fix this don't we!*

   Yes.

6. He checks the rest of the spine carefully actually marking on my back with a grease pencil the exact vertebra. Then calls them out by name as he writes them down right in front of me.

   Ok Tory, let's take a picture of this. We want an X-ray to see how much damage there is to your spine and if there is anything that might make your case more complicated. You are not a kid any more you know! Sherri will be right in to take those X-rays.

7. He's gone. Sherri comes in and click click the X-rays are done and she says: *Go ahead and put your shirt on, he'll be right back in.*

   I can hear him adjusting people as I put my shirt back on.

8. He comes back in briskly and says: *C'mon up here and let's take a look.*

   He pulls up my lumbar AP, then the lateral and says: *Remember Tory, we don't find the problem on an X-ray, I have already found the problem vertebra on _you_ a few minutes ago. The purpose of the X-ray is to determine the amount of damage your spine has and note anything that may make your case more complicated. Of course, we also note misalignments which helps us be more accurate with our care.*

   Now Tory, point to where things don't look right to you.

   Right here.

   That's right, this makes sense with what I found a minute ago.

   He explains a little more and shows a spine model so I can see exactly what the issue is. It all makes perfect sense so far.

9. Boom, out the door we go, he says: *Hey Sherri go ahead and put Tory on the IST. Tory, I will see you in a couple minutes. You are going to love this.*

10. Sherri walks me into a small room with a plain looking table and says: *Lay down with your head here, lift your knees* as she puts a knee bolster under my knees then says: *This is called an intersegmental traction table, it is a great way to stretch and mobilize the spine before you get adjusted. Just relax. It will shut off by itself and when it does just c'mon out and have a seat!*

11. Click, the table starts and I love it. I want to take it home with me.

    Click, it shuts off. I get up and go out to have a seat in a nice chair with armrests. I like it because it is not too close to anyone else.

12. Without really waiting Dr. Awesome opens his command center door, let's another happy patient out and says: *Tory c'mon in.* I walk in the room and notice a really cool glass door that I can see out of, but it is mirrored so I couldn't see in.

13. He gestures to the table and says: *Lay on your right side.* He then makes sure my positioning is perfect from feet to head, I can tell he is very systematic and thorough, making me more confident in his ability.

14. He then gives a perfect adjustment. Just the right angle, pressure, contact, stabilization, and speed. Then one more thoracic adjustment and says: *That is perfect for today Tory! You are going to love that.*

    He crumples up the face paper and tosses it into the basket across the room and turns to me saying: *Now Tory, as a DC you know you should be getting adjusted every week. I will have Sherri put you down for every Wednesday. There is no charge for today, but if you blow this off and miss a few weeks in a row, I will start charging you. Fair enough?*

    Fair enough I say and as I am walking out of the room. He, very nicely, taps me on the side of my shoulder as he says, *See you next Wednesday* then turns to his next patient and says: *Jerry c'mon back*!

15. Before I even hit the front desk Sherri says: *I have you down next Wednesday, just be here between 3 and 6.* Then looking me square in the eye as if time has stopped she says: *Do you promise to call or email me if you have to change your appointment?*

    I say *Yes.* She then unlocks her gaze and says: *Be sure to put 3:00 Wednesday and our number in your phone! Have a great day!*

    Even though she was checking in another patient she, out of one ear, heard Dr. Awesome tell me to come back next Wednesday. A proper layout and a Black Belt CA will do this.

16. I am out of there happy as can be. I literally feel the increased energy caused by the adjustment. Not one wasted second and I got exactly what I wanted, and exactly what I <u>needed</u>.

Total time in office around 15 minutes. Total patients he saw during that time was 7. Four when the X-rays were taken, two when I was on the roller table, plus me for 7 total. Everyone is happy and nobody had to wait. It was a perfect new patient experience for me as a patient.

<u>In the computer this was entered as:</u>

- 99202-25 Exam with same day adjustment $ 90
- 72040 for CT AP and Lat X-ray $100
- 72070 for TL AP and Lat X-ray $ 70
- 97012 Mechanical traction $ 30
- 98940 1-2 Region adjustment   <u>$ 50</u>

Total charge for the visit $340

My diagnosis codes in the system: M99.02 and M99.03. ICD-10. Diagnosis codes are very easy for chiropractors. There are only around 12 codes we commonly use. We have a handy sheet of what diagnosis codes to consider for all our clients. Using the right ICD-10 codes is critical.

In a typical medical office, the same level of service would be closer to $1000 and I would probably not feel any better. Chiropractic at its most expensive is still the best value EVER in health care!

Notice how much things cost for any dental or medical visit you or your family have. Read all medical type invoices and EOBs carefully to learn. (**E**xplanation **O**f **B**enefits = The letter from an insurance company showing what a doctor's office did and charged you).

Here Is the Lesson:

If you can provide what people really want you will be busy, plain and simple. If you are not busy it is because you are not offering what the masses of people really want.

Every procedure that I have and teach matches what <u>people really want.</u> Every minor step of every procedure can be either good or bad. A typical office visit to get adjusted has <u>over 40 small components</u> to get right if you want the person to come back.

Patients operate on a very simple plus or minus system. Every tiny component, every second of a visit in your office registers as either a plus or a minus. The call, the drive there, how easy to park, how far to walk in, the greeting by the CA, does the CA look healthy, the CAs mood, the temperature, smell, the sounds in the office every moment throughout the visit, the doctor's mood, image, fingernails, who else is in the office, are they annoying, the fee, the bathroom, on and on. Add it all up and there needs to be 90% pluses for them to want to come back.

I will explain it even simpler. When a patient is driving by your clinic during office hours they either register a GREEN light or a RED light. Either they want to stop in or they don't. They may not even know why on a conscious level. This is reality. We must make everything great with <u>all elements </u>in our office so when we say: *If you are ever driving by you have to stop in and get adjusted!* They will!

Your mind does exactly the same thing. Consider chiropractic offices in your area that you might visit. Do they get the green or the red light and why? How about places you like to eat, workout, or get a massage. Why do you like these places? Why do you <u>not</u> like others?

What Do We Really Sell as A Skilled and Caring Chiropractor?

Hope: For a better day, a better week, and a better life in countless ways we cannot even begin to quantify! *Chiropractic brings hope!*

Relief: Yes, we must do all we can to make patients feel better as fast as possible. This is what you would want... right? *Chiropractic brings natural relief!*

Future Academic Success: A boy is clearly in pain from a hard fall skiing. The family doctor just gave him pills. He can't do his homework because he is unable to sit and concentrate long enough to get anything done. He is falling way behind in algebra. If he doesn't learn this well it will hurt him in every math and science class he takes for the rest of his academic life.

Dad wanted nothing to do with a chiropractor, but mom finally brings the boy in to see you anyway. Several adjustments and he feels great! Fully alive, power flowing, he is back to doing well in school. He ended up getting a major academic scholarship to his local university. He, his mom, and his dad now see the chiropractor every couple weeks. What if mom never would have brought him in?

Chiropractic can save a person's academic and ultimately their income producing future!

Athletic Success: A local college athlete takes a fall. Her neck and back are killing her. The trainers give her pills. The MD sends her to Physical Therapy. *She is a high-level athlete who exercises for a living - what are more exercises going to do to help her?*

She cannot compete and misses two big track meets. It's her junior year, her scholarship and senior year are on the line, not to mention her self-esteem.

She meets a chiropractor who had a booth at a local running event. She goes in for a free evaluation. Several adjustments later she is better than she was before. She competes well in the last and most important meets of the season.

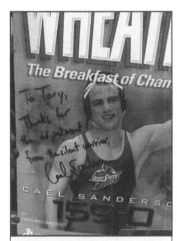

Was I part of the reason he won a gold medal and is now one of the most respected and dominating coaches in NCAA history? Obviously not, but it sure didn't hurt!

She retains her scholarship and now with regular chiropractic care is ready for a great senior year.

What if that chiropractor would not have been at that running event? What if that DC had been too lazy, scared, or tired, and not been in that booth? *Chiropractic changes athletic futures!*

Dreams: A young girl named Danielle is in dance. She loves it and is really good. Danielle has a dream of performing in front of a huge cheering crowd someday.

At age 11, Danielle notices bad hip pain to the point where she cannot do many of the moves required in her routines. It hurts all day, even sitting causes pain that is affecting her grades.

Soon, she can't practice. All she can do is show up to dance and watch all the other girls get better and leave her behind. Her parents take her to the MD and PT. The pain pills make it hurt less, but they give her diarrhea and make her feel sick.

Interestingly, one day while watching a dance practice with her parents, Danielle notices a woman walk in the door of the dance studio. The lady smiled and then turned toward the front desk. She said a few things to the lady behind the front desk, then handed her something and calmly walked out.

As practice was ending, the front desk person walked up to the hurting girl and her parents. Knowing Danielle was struggling she said: *This really nice chiropractor just dropped off her card. She said if anyone here ever has anything bugging them to call her. Maybe you should give her a try.*

The parents were able to get her in right away. Danielle went on to become the captain of one of the most decorated dance teams in the NCAAs Division I. She became a National Champion in dance and is now a cheerleader in the NFL and routinely performs in front of over 70,000 people.

The chiropractor went on to be the 'unofficial' chiropractor for all the local NFL cheerleaders. She has attracted well over 100 new patients from this exposure.

Chiropractic can make lost dreams come true!

Family: A guy gets hurt working construction. His back starts to bother him to the point where he files a Work Comp claim. He tries but he just cannot do the heavy work his job requires.

He goes to the MD and ends up with a prescription for some strong pain killers. He gets an MRI and tries some PT but it does nothing. They are now talking about doing a surgery that would have him out of work for at least three months.

His income stops and even though his wife is working they are unable to pay their bills. They also have a young son. The boy sees dad in pain, and when dad is in pain he is not very nice to be around.

This goes on for several months. Bills are now behind, the wife is stressed to the max, and the son starts to struggle in school. He is sad all the time because his dad is mean and never wants to play with him anymore.

Dad's mood is getting worse to the point where mom wonders if her marriage is over. He's now had two surgical consults that were not very convincing. It was like they didn't know what the problem really was or what to do about it.

His wife also sees he is becoming addicted to the heavy pain killers. She is very scared. One day at work, she hears her boss say that he just came from some great new chiropractor in town. She goes in to the boss's office and says: *Do you think he can help my husband?* Her boss says: *Probably, this guy seems like he can fix anything.*

She makes an appointment for her husband that day. A couple months later the chiropractor is driving past a park on his way home from work. He sees the mom and dad smiling and playing with their laughing son as they push him on a swing. The DC now takes care of all 22 employees at that business.

Chiropractic can change a family's entire future!

Opportunity: Jennifer and Claudia are the final two candidates out of 53 competing to attend Stanford and get an MBA completely paid for by their company. The company only sends one person every 4 years. Claudia is the front runner, but there is one final intense interview that this is all riding on. She has to nail this interview in front of the international board of directors to win.

Unfortunately, Claudia has been suffering from bad migraine headaches. She has missed two days of work and word is getting around that she may not be reliable. Despite the pain pills, they are not going away. She thinks: *If I have a headache the day of that interview I will have no chance.*

Five days before the final interview a friend says to her: *My chiropractor is having a Patient Appreciation Day and I can bring anyone I want. You can get a free treatment and everything that day. Why don't you come with me?*

Claudia had never been to a chiropractor but heard they can help with headaches. She agrees to go. Claudia loves it and can't believe how much better she feels after her first adjustment.

She prepays for a care plan and goes in every day until the interview. She feels better than ever and nails the interview.

She is at Stanford now getting an MBA completely paid for by her company. On top of that, she has a chiropractor there plus has a healthy raise waiting for her when she returns. ***Chiropractic saves life changing opportunities from being lost!***

Longevity: A 77 year old woman gets a hip replacement. Soon after, she starts to complain of low back pain. She goes back to her surgeon. He says it will probably go away and prescribes a painkiller. It doesn't go away. She goes back and he gives her a stronger painkiller.

The pain pills mixing with her other medication ruin her appetite. She starts to lose weight and can't walk very well at all. The pain and the sick feeling make it so she can't drive

This was 2001. Viola loved her chiropractic. It helped her so that she could see her great grandson be born and get to know him. Never underestimate the power of how chiropractic can change lives. It is utterly amazing!

a car and get around like she used to. She feels like a burden.

Her kids are very concerned. They don't want to see her suffer.

A couple months later she is clearly withering away. The surgeon says maybe he could do another surgery on her back but is reluctant because she already had a significant hip operation.

She can't walk well, drive or eat. The family feels Grandma may not make it to Christmas. Her will to live is starting to fade.

One day Grandma gets her mail and sees a post card from a local chiropractor that says: *If you donate two canned goods for our Thanksgiving Day food drive you get a free spinal exam and one complete treatment!* It also says: *We have patients that are one day old up to 99 years old!*

She asks her son and daughter if she should call. They agree to call and she gets in right away. The chiropractor took some X-rays and sees her low back was thrown-off after the surgery.

He was confident he could make adjustments to at least give her some relief. He said: *We will take as much relief as we can get as fast as we can get it!* Grandma and the daughter agreed.

That was seven years ago. Grandma is now getting around well with no sign of slowing down. She personally sees to it that everyone in her family, great grandkids included, never miss their chiropractic visits! ***Chiropractic literally saves lives.***

I can go on and on. I have had over 10,000 new patients and have stories like this for days. Improved mobility, less medical intervention, better sleep, more energy, becoming smarter, athletic achievements. Imagine the endless ways chiropractic can change a person's life!

This is what we sell! Have the lifetime vision for this. We see a patient walk in and we immediately think about how we can change their life forever! Not just in the short term with symptom relief. That is just the beginning.

We have a lifetime VISION for every person we see. We also have the VISION of the perfectly running office. We have a VISION for the perfect adjustment. We have a VISION for the ideal office visit.

A person only grows to the level of their vision. Our actions are only as good as the thoughts that govern them. What we sell is our VISION!

Much of this depends on our ability to explain chiropractic and our ability to sell chiropractic. We must study, learn, and become incredibly competent at convincing all ages of people to come to our office.

We must have excellent procedures so we can appropriately inspire as many people as we can to start and stay under care with us.

We must have office visits that are so good they literally sell every patient on coming back for their next appointment.

We must, through our confidence and capability, sell them on sending in their family and friends.

Most importantly, we must sell them on ourselves! How do we do that? It is not hard to figure out. If a chiropractor is well conditioned physically, dresses properly, has a nice office, memorizes their procedures, hires and trains a good team, interacts with other successful doctors regularly, and has a depth of belief that is contagious, there is no limit to the number of people a chiropractor may help!

When in Doubt Just Ask:

1. *What would I want myself?*

2. *If could pick any chiropractor to go to, would I pick myself?*

3. *If I had a son or daughter that became a chiropractor, would I want them to be just like me?*

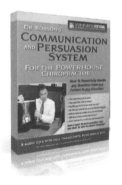

I created an audio set with the exact wording and delivery techniques to answer all the common questions that patients, people, and family will forever ask you as a chiropractor.

Many feel it is the most powerful material they have ever heard on this critical skill.

Knowing exactly what to say in every situation makes being a chiropractor so much more fun.

What Do People REALLY NEED Anyway?

- **A 44 year-old man** comes in and has some tingling in his right hand that has been getting worse for a couple months. Approximately how long and how many visits is it going to take for him to get better?

- **A 55 year-old woman** feels pretty good but has extensive spinal degeneration, what is the best recommendation for her?

- **A 62 year-old man** is 100 pounds overweight, taking 5 different medications, has severe DJD, and is a smoker. He comes to see you for low back pain. He has had the pain off and on for years. Generally, how long will it take for him to "get better?" How many visits will you recommend?

- **A 16 year-old school gymnast** comes in. She has mid and low back pain that is mild. Roughly how long will it take under care for her to get better? What will your care plan be for her? How many visits are you going to tell her parents she needs?

Do you realize that most people you see are actually suffering <u>not</u> from pain or some named condition, but from a **chiropractic deficiency** or what I call Chiropractic Deficiency Disease or CDD. I have never heard this term before, but it is so true.

A person has never been to a dentist and goes in for the first time at age 30 and needs a LOT of dental work. What is the problem? The real problem is Dental Deficiency Disease! A mental condition of not being aware, capable, or smart enough to go to the dentist regularly in the past. Same is true for the chiropractor!

- **A 43 year-old woman** who has never seen a chiropractor walks in. She is in pain. She of course asks you: *What caused this?* and *What is the problem?* Your answer is Chiropractic Deficiency Disease! She is suffering from a **chiropractic deficiency**.

If a person is horribly deconditioned what is your immediate assessment? Exercise Deficiency Disease of course! Or Nutrition Deficiency Disease.

Always feel confident enough to plainly tell people: *Mr. Jones, this is caused from spinal neglect. It is not your fault. Nowhere are we taught how important it is for everyone to get regular checkups at the chiropractor. You are suffering from a chiropractic deficiency.*

- **How about you**, yes YOU staring at this page. How often should YOU get adjusted for the rest of YOUR life? Add up how many adjustments that is?

- How many adjustments should **you** have <u>already received</u> up to this point in your life?

- **A 40 year-old man** walks in having never been to a chiro before. How many adjustments behind is he?

- **A baby is born** today and is going to live a wonderful life to 90. How many times should she get her spine checked at the chiropractor during her lifetime?

<u>**My Thoughts on the Above Questions:**</u>

Obviously, there are more questions to ask, exams to do, and possibly imaging to study for each of these but follow along for now.

- **A 44-year-old man** comes in and has some tingling in his right hand that has been getting worse for a couple of months. Approximately how long and how many visits is it going to take for him to get better?

  Consider 4 visits a week for 2 weeks, then 3 times a week for 3 months <u>minimum</u>. Once it is resolving, then back the adjusting frequency off to once a week.

  If it is all the way into his hand that means it has to heal a lot farther than just a local issue.

  Numbness, weakness, and tingling are big problems that will need adjustments and time. All the tissue cells must die off so new and better ones can replace them bringing better function.

  Of course, this case can be more complicated if it is caused from his work. If he keeps working it will take longer to get better. People have to work to survive, so we must work around this.

- **A 55 year-old woman** feels pretty good but has extensive degeneration, what is the best recommendation for her?

How she "feels" is not the primary concern. Arresting her DJD, gaining, and maintaining her mobility is the task at hand. Consider 3 visits a week for 12 weeks, then once per week forever.

One goal we always have is to keep people from ever having to use a cane, a walker, or a wheel chair. I tell this to patients.

Karen, my job is to keep you from becoming all hunched over and away from ever needing a cane, a walker, or a wheelchair!

- **A 62-year-old man** is 100 pounds overweight, taking 5 different medications, has severe DJD and is a smoker. He comes to see you for low back pain that he has had off and on for years. Generally, how long will it take for him to "get better?" How many visits will you recommend?

Adjust <u>every day</u> he can make it in for at least 3 months. Then once or twice per week forever. Plus, recommend he adopt some healthier habits. Let's be honest, there is little chance he will change his lifestyle. All you can do is the best you can with your chiropractic care and your successful, healthy attitude.

This person is so deconditioned and bogged down that their ability to heal is very low. If this person feels better at all, be glad. In many cases the goal is to keep them from getting worse.

Remember, they have years of freight train like momentum propelling their health a certain way. What does it take to slow this all down?

A freezing Minnesota day. Perfect for going in to practice scripting, make a new website video, prepare for a talk, get ready to hire a new CA, clean, touch up walls, or set updated goals.

You have to be willing to <u>work</u> if you want to achieve anything impressive.

Regular work ethic = You get average. Superior work ethic = You get everything.

Doctor, I'm really not much better and I have been here 3 months.

Yes Bill, what does that tell you about how bad your condition is?

Well doctor what are you going to do about it?

Listen Bill, it is your back and you wrecked it. This has been an issue for years. Our first job is to keep it from getting worse and you having to go in for needle injections, which will only cover up the pain while the underlying problem gets worse, or surgery which is unbelievably risky.

Be patient in a case like this. It really won't start healing until we back off on our adjusting frequency and give the tissue more time to heal between the adjustments.

Do the walking like I recommended and I will see you Monday.

- **A 16 year-old school gymnast** comes in. She has mid and low back pain that is mild. Roughly how long will it take under care for her to get better? What will your care plan be for her? How many visits are you going to tell her parents she needs?

A block of 12 visits should do well as she has super-fast tissue turnover and healing time. Three times a week for four weeks then once a week forever. More if needed when in-season, practicing, and competing in her sport.

Mom and Dad, all in-season athlete's like Lexi should be in here every week for maximum recovery and performance. Since she is in here, you might as well get tuned-up too. Mom what is it that bothers you?

Always get the parents in. Kids NEVER seem to do as well if they are taken to the doctor with a problem compared to: *We ALL go to the chiropractor together! It is good for ALL of us and makes us ALL feel and perform better!*

We are NOTHNG like the regular doctor! People go to the regular doctor for a problem. They go to the chiropractor to be their best!

- **How about you**, yes YOU staring at this page. How often should you get adjusted for the rest of your life? Add up how many adjustments that is.

If you are 25 and want to make it to age 90 that would be around 3000 adjustments.

How many adjustments should you have <u>already received</u> up to this point in your life?

If you are 25 this would be around 1000 adjustments.

- **If a 40 year-old man** walks in having never been to a chiropractor before, how many adjustments behind is he?

He is at least 1000 if not 1500 adjustments behind. Realize your 36-visit care plan over the next 90 days is nothing! It is incredible how few adjustments can make such a BIG difference. It is a phenomenon how powerful chiropractic care really is.

There are people who are in such bad shape. What they need to get healthy is beyond what their habits and self-worth may allow.

Then there are those who are competition level athletes and fitness die-hards. These men and women of all ages have chiropractic as the center of their high-performance healthy lifestyle!

Really think about this concept. If a woman is 50lbs overweight how many workouts behind is she? Thousands!

How many smaller meals behind is she? Thousands!

A man is 35 years old and is a Blue Belt in a martial art. He has a friend who is the same age but is a Black Belt. How many training sessions and competitions <u>more</u> has the Black Belt done to become a Black Belt? Thousands!

I am sitting here wishing I could play the guitar like a pro. Looking back at my life, how many guitar practices, recitals, and concerts behind am I? Thousands!

- **If a baby is born** today and was going to live a wonderful life to 90, how many times should she get her spine checked at the chiropractor during her lifetime?

Considering it would be incredible if a person could get their spine checked every week of their life, take out major holiday weeks and other missed weeks, this would be around 4000 adjustments!

So, when we make an initial plan for any patient, realize it is incredibly few visits compared to what they really need!

A minimum guideline: 12 initial visits for healthy children then wellness. 24 to 36 initial visits for adults followed by wellness.

Tissue heals about as fast as hair grows. Tissue heals as fast as fingernails grow. Think about it.

Feeling better is nice, but for all the damaged cells in the affected area to be replaced with healthy ones takes the time it takes.

If you sprain an ankle how long before it is mostly healed? If you get a bad cut that requires stitches, how long before it is mostly healed? I have noticed that after about 90 days most injuries will be mostly healed. Therefore, a care recommendation of 90 says is biologically sound.

The body must take the food we eat and turn it into new living tissue to repair the damaged area. By the time a person even feels pain there are billions of damaged cells.

Think primarily in terms of neurology and nerve flow. Some DCs are just "loosener uppers" and think chiropractic is only musculoskeletal. Many chiropractors solely focus on treating "pain and symptoms." This is not the high road in practice.

We always want patients to feel better, but understand that feeling better is actually a side effect of chiropractic.

Question: *Tory, are there any side effects to chiropractic?*

Answer: *Yes, the side effects are: Less pain, more energy, faster healing, better sleep, more mobility, less degeneration, better athletic performance, a sharper mind, more productivity at work and many other things!*

Think ORGANS and organ health! 100% nerve flow from brain going 100% to all organs 100% of the time. This is what chiropractic is all about! Think nerve flow! Think body chemistry. All chemicals in the body are created and governed by the central nerve system! When you think like this it is easy to see that everyone should have max nerve flow. Only chiropractic can affect this directly with chiropractic adjustments.

I have said many times that if heart disease is a leading cause of death, maybe we should be adjusting everyone's T1-T4 and checking their Atlas every single week. Seems obvious to me.

A vital term to learn is this: As a chiropractor you are simply a **casual observer of the facts.** You are not a lawyer for your patients. You are a professional care provider with a valid opinion.

We care, but just the same we simply gather information as a casual observer and report it to people as a casual observer would. We NEVER take a patient's problem upon ourselves or "feel" too much. We must stay clear minded, objective, "teflon coated" and be a casual observer. By understanding this, we can honestly tell people what the best plan is for them based on the information available.

Many doctors recommend only what they feel people will mentally handle. They compromise their doctoring. They are unable to be a cool, objective doctor who is simply a casual observer and reporter of the facts. We have no control over how people process what we say

Our job and responsibility is to be accurate in our thoughts, words and actions with all patients at all times.

Don't give up or you will never know what might have been.
Every champion was once a beginner... that didn't quit.
- Aly Raisman
Olympic Gold Medalist

We are all used to seeing the pretty competition pictures, but the one on the bottom is the one that counts. The day in and day out grinding, hard, painful work on both good days and bad. That's what it's all about. *Are you willing to do the work to become a champion level chiropractor?*

We love you and we can help you!

These are the words you train your mind to <u>automatically think every time a person walks through your door</u>! This is the best practice building advice I could give you. It creates the correct state of mind.

It has been said that those who become super successful do so because they are able to manage their "state." We must think what we are supposed to be thinking when we are supposed to be thinking it!

We love you and we can help you!

<u>We Are Promoting Four Different Things:</u>

We are promoting *Chiropractic*: *How good are you at getting people to understand chiropractic?*

To get good at this, every doctor must know exactly how to explain chiropractic in many different ways, including being able to draw it out. We have what we call the *How Chiropractic Works* diagram. When we draw this diagram, it leaves people with no other choice than to understand and believe in chiropractic.

Knowing chiropractic history, chiropractic philosophy, anatomy, biology, and physiology are critical. You must understand chiropractic deeply enough so that when you explain it <u>people will believe you</u>. You must know your stuff. You must **be the real thing**.

We recommend you ALWAYS have your *Netter Anatomy* handy. I have the key pages marked so I can quickly show patients. They may not always believe what you SAY, but they will believe what they SEE in an anatomy book.

Me using my *Netter* again. I have had this book for over 25 years now. It never lets me down when I need people to understand how chiropractic works! When a patient understands more, they want care more. This is the starting point for great results.

Everyone can tell if you are *into* your work. There is no way to fake it if you aren't. People LOVE to go to those who are *into* their work. I am *into* chiropractic and chiropractic is *into* me!

We love you and we can help you!

We are promoting *Our Office*: *How good are you at getting people to believe that your office is the place to go above all other choices?*

This is normally done without words. The way we promote our office is by having a great design in an accessible location. A well branded and placed office sells itself.

When a person walks into an office and sees a board packed with happy patient pictures and Thank You's, it is as if you are saying: *Of course you want to come here, everybody loves to come here.*

People buy with their eyes. Always remember that. *People buy with their EYES.* What they SEE is more important than what you say. Chiropractors are always asking me what to say. This makes little difference if people don't already like what they SEE.

What do they SEE when they look at you and your office?

Office 1: See a chewed-up parking lot, dirty entryway, front door with no decals, soiled and crooked mats, front desk with stuff everywhere, and a CA who looks a little rough and doesn't even stand or smile. There is no music - the place is like a morgue. No referral board. Hardly any chiropractic anything anywhere and a the place smells old. You notice typical gossip magazines loaded with drug ads on a table, some with curled up corners. Then the doctor appears looking a little sloppy, tired, and out of shape..

Office 2: A clean parking lot, spotless entryway, nice clinic logo and an office hours decal on the door, spotless mats and a healthy looking CA who stands and smiles. The front desk is organized with no clutter anywhere. It is bright, smells nice, with neutral music, impressive diplomas all hung neatly. There is a full referral board, chiropractic posters everywhere, and a chiropractic video silently playing on a TV with no cords visible. A Chiropractic Health and Wellness magazine is sitting on every chair. Then a physically conditioned and very well-dressed doctor with great posture appears. The doctor has a very cool and capable demeanor, smiling warmly and confidently.

Which one are you going to be? *You must have an office that promotes you, your care, and chiropractic!*

Any website or social media must also have great pictures. The pictures must show you and your office as inviting. In the great book *Psycho Cybernetics* by Maxwell Maltz we learn: ***Image is ALL.***

We love you and we can help you!

We are promoting our *Recommendations*: *How good are you at getting people to start care? How good are you at getting people to follow and complete the treatment plans you recommend?*

> **Question:** What is going to be your initial recommendation of care for most adult patients you see? In other words, how many visits are you going to recommend for adults, most of the time?

> **Question:** How long does it usually take ligaments, tendons, muscles, bones and nerves to heal?

> **Question:** Are you just going to be a pain doctor? Are you only seeking for patients to get superficial results and "feel" better?

> **Question:** Are you going to make care plans that will actually be long enough to bring a more thorough healing?

> **Question**: Do you want people and families to continue to come in and see you for ongoing wellness care?

> **Question**: After an initial care plan, what will your wellness options be? What will they cost?

> **Question**: If a patient wants to see you every two weeks for a year, what will it cost if they prepay? What if they pay monthly?

> **Question**: What if a person wants to come in once a month and asks to prepay for a year, how much will it cost? What if this person wants to pay monthly? How much if they pay per visit?

Question: A mom loves chiropractic and your office. She wants her entire family to be able to come in whenever they want. She wants to buy unlimited visits for her family of 6. How much will this cost per year? How much if she wants to auto-pay monthly?

The point I am making here is: *You must know what you are selling.* We recommend you offer initial care plans to all patients. **A solid starting point for an initial recommendation for an adult is 90 days**. Then as initial care is winding down we have a very specific procedure to get the person to want ongoing care in a wellness plan.

We have all the details for creating initial plans for cash, insurance, Medicare, personal injury and workers comp patients. It would take another book for me to explain these. The art of making care plans and presenting them is one of the most vital skills a chiropractor can master.

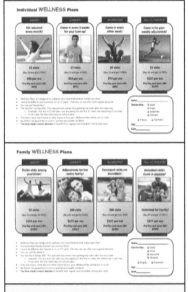

Individual and Family Wellness Plans. Ours will accommodate any person or family who wants wellness care. They are difficult to create since every level must have correct pricing. We have never seen anyone with smarter plans than these.

We also have all the wellness plans for individuals and for families already created with all prepay and auto pay fees engineered. We have a 10 video training series for our clients on how to become a Black Belt at this.

One of the biggest problems in the profession today is chiropractors who are afraid to tell people the truth. There are many reasons for this.

Reason 1: Laziness, lack of study, or lack of good coaching. They may not know what the truth is or what the correct treatment plan should be.

Reason 2: They are fearful and want patients to like them. They sugar coat their report and make a recommendation they *hope* their patients will accept.

Reason 3: The doctor has a personality where they want to try and always give good news and make others happy. This makes it difficult for them to tell the truth when it is required.

Are you afraid to tell people the truth? Are you going to be a real doctor? One who listens carefully, evaluates thoroughly, then makes a smart and appropriate recommendation based on facts, objective findings, anatomy, biology, and physiology?

If we love and care about people we will tell them the truth.

The real doctor, the real expert, the real pro knows the truth or at least has an intelligent opinion. Then communicates it in a nice way.

We love you and we can help you!

We are promoting *Ourselves. How good are you at getting people to listen to YOU, believe in YOU, and look up to YOU for health advice?*

If you want to know the answer to this just look at your PVA and Patient Referrals each month. How many visits on average does a person come see you in their lifetime? This tells you how much people like you, your care, your office, your fees, your everything.

How many patients are excited enough about your care to tell others to come see you? A doctor with a PVA of 9 and only 2 referrals a month probably should not be talking about how great they are.

A doctor with a PVA of 44 and over 20 referrals every month doesn't have to say anything!

Our focus as doctors of chiropractic is to become incredibly good at promoting our profession, our office, our care, and ourselves! Your ability to do this completely controls your income. Whether a person believes it or not, it is a fact that whatever controls your income controls your life.

It is fairly easy to keep score as a chiropractor. When we want to know the truth about how well we are doing in practice, all we have to do is look at our stats. Numbers reveal the truth.

Question: Which of the following doctors is <u>more</u> successful?

DC #1: Pays $2500 a month for marketing.
Gets 40 new patients per month.
5 of the new patients are from referrals.
Has a PVA of 11 visits.

DC #2: Does no marketing.

Gets just 20 new patients per month.

17 of the new patients are from referrals.

Has a PVA of 44 visits.

DC #1 has 40 new ones x 11 PVA = **440** total visits.

DC #2 has 20 new ones x 44 PVA = **880** visits.

Despite getting half as many new patients, DC #2 is TWICE as busy as DC #1 and pays <u>nothing</u> to get new patients. DC #1 is trying to "buy" new patients with marketing because they can't generate any referrals.

Not to mention DC #2 is getting 17 sweet referrals. Be aware of how much doctor and staff time 40 new patients takes. How much of it is wasted on those who don't start care?

DC #2 is more efficient and spends half as much time processing new patients yet sees <u>twice</u> the volume and collects <u>twice</u> as much. Notice too, with an overhead of $2500 less! This is the WINNERS**EDGE** way!

You must assume that DC #2 has better systems, image, care, and smarter recommendations. The doctor has all the elements that count in the eyes of a patient. The question we ask is: *Are you referable?*

Considerations in Filling Up the Practice:

- Success in practice is largely a popularity contest. Always has been, is now, and always will be. You need to shake hands with 1500 to 3000 people as fast as you can. This ensures a good start.

Tory, how do I do that? You THINK. Go anywhere people are, stick out your hand and as you shake their hand you say: *Hey I'm Dr. Healthy, if anything is ever bothering you give me a call!*

I was asked a few years ago: *Tory, if you came to my office what all would you do to grow to 100 patients a day?* What a smart question! Ten hours of audio later here it is. Our ***Practice Promotion Mastery***. *How to get to 100 patients a day in 90 days or less.*

120

There are so many things you can do to become well known in your area. I can only introduce a few here.

Do you realize that all the new patients you get are simply a % of the number of people that you know? If you want more new ones, you have to meet and know more people. This is another reason why we ALWAYS recommend you live close to your office.

We love you and we can help you!

- Be a nice, likable, agreeable, good person. This along with telling the truth in a caring way = A big practice!

- Friends and family will want to come see you. *What do you charge them?* Learn this line: EVERYBODY PAYS.

- If you have a large family and marry a person from the area who also has a large family, you could be seeing 20 or more visits a week of free visits. Add up the lost money here: 20 x $40 per visit x 50 weeks a year = $40,000 in lost collections every year.

All friends and family MUST be told that a visit costs money. It costs you about $24 in overhead to see a human being in your office. If you give a visit away for free it is NOT free. It costs YOU $24. Do they own a business where you can walk in and get everything for free? People love free stuff – until it is time for them to give free stuff away.

Imagine you own a pizza place. People would understand that a pizza costs money to make: Dough, sauce, toppings, prep time, and oven time. It is harder to understand that your SERVICE also costs money.

Any family member or friend who expects anything for free should be ashamed and embarrassed for their selfishness and total lack of respect for you, your business, and your time. Since your life is made up of only time, it's a lack of respect for you.

Only a very self-centered, "cheap," disrespectful person would expect you to see them for free. If they are a decent family member or a real friend they will ALWAYS want to pay you out of respect. I promise you they would want you to pay them.

Some will want to come in all the time. Other family and friends will never come see you. Be okay with this.

No lazy care with these people. Always do a full exam and make a full recommendation. If they do not agree to it, <u>don't see them</u>! I guarantee you will thank me for this. Those family or friends that you let in easy will walk all over your schedule. They will never listen to you, not refer anyone, and cost you more than it's worth. Be smart here.

Lines to consider:

- *Can I come to where <u>you</u> work for free?*

- *I have to charge you at least what it costs me to see you, and that is $25.*

- *This business is expensive to run and you are here in place of someone who would pay $50. So how much should I charge you?*

- *This is a business. I <u>personally</u> want to see everyone for free but owning a business doesn't work that way.*

- *Being my buddy, here's the deal: If you pay for 12 visits I will give you 24.*

- *Our really cool family and friend policy is $25 per visit.*

- *My policy is: We will use your insurance if you have any. Otherwise we have a cash deal of $25 per visit. If you miss or don't follow the plan and just want to walk in whenever you are in crisis to use chiropractic like an aspirin, it will be our regular fee of $70 per visit.*

- *Does the owner of a grocery store let his family and friends get free food whenever they feel like it?*

- *Does a personal trainer give family and friends free private training sessions and lose the $100 per hour that they could have made on a legit client?*

- *We have a family and friend policy of $25 per visit, but if you have Medicare we must use that. If you get in a car or work injury we will also use the appropriate insurance.*

We love you and we can help you!

- This brings up one of many points. Let's say you are giving office visits to a friend for free. He's a buddy so you are not doing a full SOAP note on every visit. After many visits over a couple years he unfortunately gets in an auto accident. He was not at fault and was significantly injured. He hired an attorney right away. You keep seeing him and start doing a real SOAP note on every visit. You also start to bill his insurance.

A few weeks into care the at-fault insurance company and both attorneys request all patient records for this person. <u>All</u> records from the very first day he came in. They absolutely have the right to request these, and you absolutely have to provide them.

They notice there were a lot of visits, not very good notes, missing notes, and no charges for any of the prior care.

Later, the lead attorney for the insurance company confronts you during a two-hour video deposition: *Doctor, records indicate the same care prior to the accident was free, but now you want to charge $70 per visit. Why exactly is this doctor?*

Also, doctor please direct your attention to pages 53 to 67 in front of you. Are those your notes for this patient doctor? Why is it doctor that your notes prior to the incident are incomplete and some dates are missing, but after the accident the notes appear complete? Doctor, is it not your responsibility to have a complete note on each and every visit? Please notice we have your State Board rules for documentation. Will you please read aloud paragraph 4, section 3 for all of us.

You get demolished and embarrassed during the deposition. You have no credibility and anything you say at this point is discounted. Your friend's attorney is anything but happy as his case may suffer. Getting all the doctor bills paid and a favorable settlement for his client may be compromised by you.

This case ends up going to court. You are put on the stand. Jurors are staring at you. Attorneys are staring at you. Your friend and his entire family in the crowd are staring at you.

Your credibility again gets demolished. You, your care, your office, and your entire profession is discredited because of your violation of Board rules for documentation. In addition, and even more damning, is the clear appearance that you are attempting to gouge the insurance company. You are charging them thousands for the same care that the same person was paying nothing for a couple months ago.

Even though there were some stronger witnesses, the damage is done. You tarnish the entire case costing your friend tens of thousands in lost settlement money.

You get paid barely 20% of what you billed. Your friend no longer comes to see you. In fact, he doesn't even talk to you anymore. The attorney and many others never send you another referral. The insurance companies involved decide to place under investigation any bills you send them in the future.

Feeling very small you just can't figure it out. You thought you were being "nice" and being "cool" by bending and letting a friend come in casually. You find yourself recalling famous sayings like: *Nice guys finish last* and *It doesn't pay to be nice.*

Integrity fills up a practice:

- Fact is: By giving care away and being sloppy you are NOT being nice to your family and friends.

- If they don't think your care is worth paying for, then are they really your friends?

The most successful investor and possibly most efficient money handler in American history is the great Warren Buffet. In making hiring decisions he says he looks for three things: **Integrity Intelligence** and **Energy**. These simple criteria are genius. They also determine how successful any chiropractor will be.

- Do you have integrity?
- How intelligent are you?
- How much energy do you have?

Every person's life is a clear outward display of these three inner qualities.

- Treat everyone well and maintain integrity with patients via complete care, full exams, SOAP notes and fair payment plans.

- Notice when you get sloppy YOU are the one who ends up paying.

- Have a standard in your office. *I will do this, but I won't do that.* Sometimes these are called boundaries. I'd rather just call them procedures to follow. Just like every other business does.

- Notice how many successful businesses are franchises. Orange Theory, McDonalds, Jiffy Lube, and Dairy Queen are all franchises. Why are they so successful? They have rules and procedures that are followed to the letter or the franchisee gets their franchise shut down. Nobody will shut us down, so we have to create, follow and enforce our procedures ourselves.

- NEVER be afraid, or more positively stated, ALWAYS tell people the truth and maintain a standard in your office.

- Except in the rarest of circumstances I would never adjust anyone outside my office. My saying: *I don't do shoddy work. You want my best care so come to my office on Monday!*

- Or even: *We are working on the vertebra that protect and affect your spinal cord and nerve system that runs your body. Come to my office on Monday and we will do it right!*

- You would never ask a dentist to grab a fork and look in your mouth while watching a ballgame at a friend's house, would you?

- Chiropractors are notorious for bastardizing and diminishing the value of chiropractic and the adjustment by "adjusting" people everywhere. I have even seen drunk people out boating with some chiropractor there "adjusting" people trying to look cool. Chiropractic is not a party trick.

- In school, chiropractic students are throwing chiropractic around everywhere. We must always respect and have reverence for our incredible art and its incredible power.

- I recommend all *party trick, show off, shoddy, and poorly thought-out* care END when you graduate. Better yet, never let it start.

- Decide right now to become a real chiropractor who takes chiropractic and their reputation seriously.

Lesson from *The Master Key* by Charles Haanel 1916

"We make money by making friends and we enlarge our circle of friends by making money for them, by helping them, by being of service to them. The first law of success is then service, and this in turn is built on integrity and justice. The person who is not fair in their intention is simply ignorant. They have missed the fundamental law of all exchange, they are impossible, they will lose surely and certainly.

They may not know it, they may think they are winning, but they are doomed to certain defeat. Nobody can cheat the infinite. The Law of Compensation will demand of us an eye for an eye and a tooth for a tooth."

The Master Key. I place it in the top 3 of the most important success writings in history. Every chiropractor who wants to be an ultra-success should study it. Don't just read it, STUDY it. I have been studying it over and over for 9 years now. I never stop learning from it. Once I am done I go back and start reading it again.

Many ask me: *Tory what is a good new book to read?*

Answer: *It is not about new books, it is about studying and deeply understanding just a few books. The Master Key Is one of them.*

My home command center. Notice the arrow pointing to The Master Key. I use a PDF copy so I can focus solely on one page at a time and write notes. The home command center is a place to get mental work done. A place to work on <u>your mind</u>. The place from which you CREATE and direct your life. Some call it an office or a study.

Observation: The biggest thing in a poor person's house is usually their TV. The biggest thing in a rich person's house is their pile of books and success material.

- When someone is in trouble they will need a REAL chiropractor. Someone who takes their craft <u>seriously</u>. A person who will analyze carefully, listen, and deliver **really good** adjustments!

- There are two scales in adjusting, one for the difficulty of the technique and another for how good the adjustment was, sort of like Olympic diving. The diver gets scored on how well executed the dive is and how hard the dive was to perform. The best execution of the most difficult dive always wins.

- You make a SOAP note for everyone on every visit, including staff. When they get in a crash, and they all seem to sooner or later, the insurance companies and attorneys will be asking for records. Always have all required records for every patient.

You be the Coach:

A DC calls you: *I just had a patient come in. He wants me to send him an invoice every month so he can come in later and pay with cash.*

Your answer?

My answer: *Uh, this is not a payment option. Our payment options are:*

1. *Pay in full with debit card, credit card, or check. You can normally offer an administrative savings discount.*

2. *Have a card on file and pay monthly starting today. We offer an administrative savings discount for this commitment also.*

3. *Pay per visit. No discount as there is no reason to give one.*

Sending bills to patients is a procedure that died over 20 years ago. We never do this unless a patient has their auto-pay fail. If this happens we send a bill and call them immediately.

Never accept payments from PayPal, Venmo or SquareCash. These apps are for person to person transactions only. Never business.

Example: 24 visit plan costs $1200. $960 if prepay.

$1060 if auto pay.

$50 per visit if paid per visit.

Those you bend rules for are the ones who make a mess in your office. Remember – being too nice usually backfires. A weird law of life.

- Family, friend, total stranger, whoever, the system and policies are the same for all. I promise the State Board, Attorney General, and Department of Commerce will expect this to be the case. They don't care if a patient is a friend, your sister, or your neighbor.

- There are many scenarios here that all have a different solution. Just know that everyone you see must know that your time and office cost money and they should never expect anything for free, from you or anyone else.

- The real winner never expects or even wants anything for free from anyone. Feeling entitled is a horrible way to live.

- Nobody owes you ANYTHING other than respect. You certainly don't owe anybody anything other than respect either.

- EVERYBODY PAYS!

- Everybody gets a SOAP note on every visit.

- Everybody's services get entered in the computer every visit.

- Run an extremely clean, organized, tight ship.

- You will only grow to your level of organization.

- Another great person to learn from is the late Jim Rohn. His audio and video materials are a standard in the success world. He was labeled America's foremost business philosopher. I love his wise saying: *Keep strict accounts!* - **Jim Rohn**

  A teenager was at a Jim Rohn Seminar years ago. He loved it and eventually started working for Jim. This young man then started his own seminars. He ended up becoming the now famous and ultra- successful Tony Robbins.

  Jim Rohn himself was a product of a man named Earl Shoaff. Rohn gives Shoaff all the credit for his success. I will also have him listed in the success resources section at the end of the book.

- Your procedures are your promotions. Every procedure should be so good it makes a patient want to tell their family and friends to come see you.

- Everywhere you go is opportunity. **ABP** = Always Be Promoting!

- Every state has rules regarding payments and prepays. Know yours before you start!

- Your mission is to tell people about chiropractic, your office, and what chiropractic can do for them. Prove that YOU are the person to see!

- Your mission is about THEM not about you.

- Most struggling DCs are fixated in a weak state of thinking only of what *they* want and what *they* supposedly "need." It is a sickening state of *me me me*. The powerhouses on the other hand, have everything geared to deliver quality to PATIENTS. They prepare themselves and their office for PATIENTS. They have a mission to reach and serve lots of PATIENTS!

Look who is up and cranking away again.

DC: *But Tory, I don't seem to have time to do all the stuff you recommend?*

Me: *Please don't lie to me. Maybe you are simply too lazy and comfort-seeking to get up and get it done.*

- Your goal is to be recognized everywhere. You want people saying nice things about you or at least knowing of you. *Hey, there's that chiropractor guy again.* Or if you are out in public someone might say: *Oh, you're that chiropractor from down the street!*

- Jim Parker, the founder of Parker Chiropractic College and Parker Seminars had a famous saying: **LSIMFT.** What does it mean?

- *Loving Service Is My First Technique!*

- It was true then and is <u>even more true now!</u>

- Some doctors are trying to make friends with their patients. These doctors think: *If I am really nice to my patients and maybe if I supplicate and spend extra time with them they will like me and want to be my friend.* This is not what builds a great office.

  People want an objective smart DOCTOR, not another friend. We do things right and make <u>great patients</u>! Do this and I promise you will have friends for life.

- Patients want you to be "above" them. They want a smart, fearless chiropractor to look up to as a health expert. Be one!

How it works:

I started in practice and worked my way in to do a talk for the HOSA club at the local high school. HOSA = Health Occupations Students of America. This resulted in my getting a few new patients.

I also volunteered every Friday morning to read stories to kids at a day care a couple blocks from my office, bringing me at least 20 new patients. Kids knew me, the teachers knew me, and parents were starting to know about me.

Within two years we had the head football coach, assistant head football coach, head basketball coach, assistant head basketball coach, the principal, the vice principal, the quarterback of the football team, the star women's basketball and softball player, the state champion golfer, two of the captains of the basketball team plus countless other friends, boyfriends, girlfriends, and parents all as patients.

I could walk into this local high school on any day and see at least 5 kids walking around wearing my T-shirt. Nothing could stop the momentum now. I had endless new patients for life.

Really think about how amazing this is. Go try to do this at your local high school.

I have said for some time: One way to tell how successful a DC is: Ask how many patients they have at their local high school. The local high school is an epicenter of massive activity in most towns.

It ALL happened because I was fearless and GAVE sincerely.

This grew to college athletes and countless professional athletes from Pro Beach Volleyball to the NFL. My favorite sport is Ultimate Fighting. I have now adjusted UFC Champions and am preparing another right now for his first title fight.

I do much less of this now because it was starting to take too much time away from my practice and consulting. I have to stay on my MISSION. Things will try to distract you, sometimes really cool and fun things, but we must stay on mission!

Your 90 Day Practice Explosion Checklist!

Growing a practice requires a MASSIVE physical and mental effort. MUCH MORE than most think. It requires that you read more chiropractic and success material than ever, listen to audios more than ever, watch videos more than ever, and attend more seminars and trainings than ever.

Whatever you might be thinking right now – quadruple it and you are getting close to the effort I'm describing. Building a practice is a 6am to 11pm day after day, week after week, month after month project.

This is why being on a MISSION and truly having a PURPOSE with a clear VISION of what you want to build is the charge that will drive you.

No drive = No practice. **BIG** drive = **BIG** practice!

- You must clearly and relentlessly picture your practice the way you want it, only then can you create it.

- In a sense, it is as simple as meeting more people, looking right and speaking well when you do.

- Your patient base is simply a percentage of the number of people that know you and think of you as a credible and desirable person to seek for health advice. Be this person.

- Take the time and effort to make yourself physically and mentally superior. People will naturally want to be around you. Some find it very easy to grow a practice. Some are always crying for how to "get more new ones." Have a personality where people just like being around you!

- The more popular you are in a positive way, the busier you will be. This cannot be emphasized enough.

- The doctor that practices where they know the most people has it MUCH easier if their approach and reputation are positive.

- The doctor who moves to where they don't know anyone is going to have to hustle. It can be done! I have done it myself many times.

- I'll say it again: A new doctor must make 1500 to 3000 eyeball to eyeball handshake contacts to get started. (I have a DC friend who knocked on 11,000 doors prior to opening. He now sees 200 patients a day.)

Right away:

1. Every night before going to bed, and every morning, sit with your eyes closed and visualize patients in your appointment book. Picture people coming in, the phone ringing, people paying, people smiling, lots of patient files, and all the chairs filled. See many types of patients in your office getting great results.

   If you can visualize them clearly you can have them. If you can visualize your office exactly the way you want it, you can create it. This is a law of success.

2. See yourself happy and doing what you want in your practice. ALL success starts with your ability to actually picture what you want. *If you can see it clearly – you can create it!*

   We love you and we can help you!

3. Complete the WINNERSEDGE Practice Transformation Guide and all our high-level doctor training videos.

4. Read all the essential books on the **Success Resources List.**

5. Get your physical training program in order. Eat what you are supposed to eat and be a physical example!

6. Every night listen to your **Success Recording.** This is a recording that you make in your own voice. It includes all your carefully engineered goals and affirmations for you, your office, and your life. It is miraculous in its power. We have a template and procedure on exactly how to make this. *You must re-program your mind to the new level. We all must if we want to grow!*

Key points:

- A doctor will grow to their ability to sit and **plan**, to take a blank piece of paper and write out the **plan** for the day, week, month, year. The best planners who take action will prosper.

- Some DCs will think their Coach or Consultant should do their thinking for them. Wrong. All doctors who want to be successful know how to sit and make a plan to reach a goal. The coach already knows how and should be able to teach you. It is one of the most powerful skills you can possess.

- Just like a dog must be TRAINED to do a trick, a doctor must be TRAINED to speak and act in such a way that people will want to come in for care. **Training training training** + Natural ability + Effort = Success.

- All the super successes in any field are the people who have the ability to make a plan, then do whatever it takes to go for it.

- Every doctor has opportunities in their area that must be found and pursued. You must examine everything within 10 miles of your office and see the opportunities. They are there! If a doctor likes bowling, joining a few bowling leagues can mean a TON of new patients. What do you like to do? Get involved. If you say *I don't really do much* then it's time to wake up and LIVE. Start doing stuff!

- Get out and do all the things you weren't able to do in school: Golf league, curling league, dart league, billiards, runs, fitness competitions, softball, teach gymnastics to kids, take Jiu Jitsu classes, whatever! Any one thing can be a big practice builder!

- The more uncomfortable you feel, the better it will work because you are stretching yourself!

- Interesting fact: The most successful DCs I coach never ask how to get more new patients. This is because they naturally attract them. Make yourself of similar magnetism.

Now let's get to work!

❑ Print 1000 - 3000 **New Patient Generators (NPGs)** exactly as we teach. Personally, and cheerfully walk into EVERY business within several miles and hand them out. This is awesome as you are finally on your mission to change the world and reach people! The goal is to walk into <u>at least</u> 200-400 businesses. Drive ten minutes in every direction from your office. Walk in to all businesses in that radius!

I have had countless chiropractors on the phone complain that they do not have many new patients. I bet I can walk across the street from their office, stroll into any business and ask: *Hey do you know that chiropractor over there across the street?* And they will say NO.

The chiropractor with endless new patients, walk anywhere around their office and EVERYONE knows who they are and likes them.

Some doctors are weak, afraid, and too self-absorbed to go out and meet people. Get excited to walk into businesses and introduce yourself. You will always get what you have earned. If you can do it – you win. If you are too weak to get out there and do it – you lose.

- Are you weak?
- Are you afraid to introduce yourself?
- Are you afraid to tell total strangers of all ages and economic levels who you are and what you do?
- Are you afraid to have a few people blow you off and say things like: *I would never go to a chiropractor!*

It is easy to answer these questions while you are kicking back reading this book. What matters is what your stats reveal about you after you open your practice. The numbers will show the truth about you. The most assertive chiropractor is usually the busiest chiropractor.

I'm repeating myself, but it must be said again: The more you do what is uncomfortable – the more successful you will be.

❑ Go to local neighborhoods to do the same. Be very casual and super nice. If people blow you off – big deal. You only care about those who are interested. Your goal is to simply meet people and put a MAJOR vibe out. The more physical effort you put in to promoting yourself the bigger your harvest will be.

❑ Get a list of 1000 businesses and engage our weekly mailing plan of sending NPGs to at least 150 businesses every week.

❑ You want everyone in the world to know where you are, what you are doing, and that you are EXCITED about it. Reason: the more people you can get thinking about you creates a magnetic power towards you. Send a letter and a business card to EVERYONE you know in the United States and beyond.

All past teachers you liked, neighbors, old coaches, bosses, family friends, your DC friends, <u>everyone</u> regardless of where they live. You must let EVERYONE know where you are and what you are doing. It does not matter if they are in another city! Just do it.

Make sure anything you send has good pictures and a good map.

A complete website with a home page video, and all social media should be up and current. Never promote until you are current online.

I have seen doctors promote, but when people go to find them online it says: *Website Under Construction.* We call this a FAIL!

❑ You can do NPG inserts in a local weekly paper. One each week for 4 weeks if possible. There are still many that read the local paper.

❑ Call ALL local family and friends. Yes, EVERYONE you know. Literally tell them to come see your new office. Check their spines while they are there!

We love you and we can help you!

❑ Set up screening-type sessions at grocery stores, gyms, health stores, bowling alleys, and shopping malls. Literally walk right in and say *Where's the manager?* Arrange one day a week for 8 – 12 weeks. Offer sheets and chair massage are best. Also, you can also simply stand there and give the offer sheet or NPG. We recommend a small fee for the first visit and donate any money collected to a local charity.

❑ Attend local fairs, trade shows, home and garden shows, and running events. Look up events by the name of the location that holds them. If there is a YMCA look up YMCA events in your town. If there is an expo hall or convention center look-up ALL the events there. Car shows, horse shows, boat shows, bridal shows, hunting expos, parades, holiday events, anything is a possibility. I've done them all!

❑ Join a fitness center and go to CLASSES at least 3 days a week. CLASSES are where you can meet people without looking like a vulture. CLASSES are where the new patients are. Trust me – they are waiting for you! I personally recommend at least 10 visits to the gym every week. Yes, even go twice a day, one AM and one PM. Consider joining <u>two or three</u> gyms to increase your reach.

- This may sound odd but go to local happy hours at all the popular places. NO drinking. Go every week until you know people there. This is where "doing it" people hang out. You are there to make a ton of friends. This is a huge source of new friends and patients. Get popular in a positive way. Don't stay too long. Go with friends whenever possible. They can endorse you!

- Start a professionally done Facebook Ad. This must be done right and include pictures or a video. Be prepared with all marketed patients to pre-qualify them when they come in. When a marketed person comes in, after the consultation stop and say: *Now John, is your health and this problem enough of a priority that if I find something I can help you with, are you planning on following my recommendations?* Then be quiet and wait for them to respond.

  You will learn if they are just there to get checked or if they really want to get better. Follow our protocol and verbiage for the predictable responses people will give you. Always be super nice!

- Go IN for everything: Gas, banking, everywhere and give out business cards! Walk in everywhere and as you interact with anyone give a card. Go to a different teller each time at the bank, never use the drive thru. Go to a different check out person at the grocery store. Give them all a card. Do this EVERYWHERE.

- Go out on the weekends. You are in socializing mode however you can do it. You will be surprised how far people will drive to see you if they like you. If not, they can refer to you. I still get referrals from people I met out years ago. Make friends and get out doing things. If married – go out and do things. There are no new patients at home!

- Memorize our referral statements and use them every day. Read them out loud at every Team Meeting.

- On every report mention you can add additional family members. This is called "parlay." Take one new patient and turn them into more.

- Make sure your website has good testimonials and pictures. Look at mine for an example; *prospinehealth.com*

❑ Good business cards + Good website with video + Promo to get people to your site = Good things for you.

❑ Make sure all online directories are complete and accurate, including Wellness.com and Healthgrades.com. You must be easy to find if a prospect is looking for you.

❑ Get the WINNERSEDGE *Technique Mastery* DVD Set. Attend an additional 1-2 technique seminars ASAP. Become a better chiropractor – this <u>always</u> works.

❑ Go to coffee shops and hang out a few times per week. Goal is to meet at least one new person each time. Read, work on a laptop, or watch WE videos. Make friends, give cards, and set appointments!

❑ Take packs of NPG to all local apartment complexes for them to give to new tenants. They love this.

❑ EVERY day make a list of what to get done that day in order to meet more people. Fill it EVERY day with action!

❑ Of course, have all scripts and systems in place. Marketing is of little use if you and your office are not ready.

❑ Flood your mind with new patient thinking. This is why we have new patient affirmation audios. They get you absorbed with thinking about new patients. **Think** new patients + **Love** new patients = **Get** more new patients. *Worrying about new patients = Few new patients.*

❑ Call and set up at least two attorney lunches per week. We have an attorney lunch video for our members. Get the **PI Mastery Set** if you want to see more PI. Do the marketing project included in the set.

❑ Visit all daycares, dental offices, gymnastic studios, dance studios, everything! What appeals to you? You must figure out the way to "make it" in your area. What is available to you? What do you like? What is around you? There is always a way to win!

❑ As volume grows, of course have a PAD as taught twice a year.

❑ If you have the space, do in-office talks. Expect 10% of your weekly volume to attend. Example: If you are seeing 200 a week you should be able to pull 20 people in for a talk. No talks are necessary to build a practice, but if you like doing them (and I have done a ton of them), start with 4 per year with exciting topics.

❑ Go visit a couple patients where they work each week. Ask when they are in and get the green light to stop by for a quick tour. Be genuinely interested. I have sparked many great NPs from this.

❑ Make a flyer saying you do FREE Lunch and Learn/Health talks in schools, daycares, or any business. List the topics you speak on.

You must be able to sit, think and create the details for any program you might want to do. We have the perfect talk in video form to study.

We love you and we can help you!

❑ Do everything locally: Cleaners, haircuts, insurance agent, oil changes, and getting gas (always go in and meet the cashier), shopping, and lunches (go to different places and give a card to ALL wait staff). Use this language: *Come in and see me, there's no charge to get checked since you work here!*

❑ Make referrals to friends, patients, and other DCs. Refer your doctor friends for coaching. The more success you bring to others, the more success you receive in return. Another natural law!

❑ Do you have a dog? Go to dog parks and give out cards. Get out there!

❑ The best marketer wins. This means getting very good at making promo pieces of any kind. I typed this book and inserted all pictures. I can make great flyers for my practice. This is a valuable skill.

❑ Are you into yoga or working out? Become an instructor and teach a couple classes a week at a busy yoga studio or gym. MANY new patients are here. You are automatically credible as an instructor.

❑ A Telemarketing blast is good to do once. Especially if new!

Now...

❑ Let any charities you may give a donation to know your plan. Set the precise date to end any promotions and always give them the money.

❑ Have all forms, employees, systems, and the office ready for new patients and ACTION! You get what you are ready and prepared for.

❑ Review at the team meeting so all are on board. If you don't have staff, get someone – you will need them.

❑ Adjust invisible patients in downtime. This is key – you MUST do this to create the "vacuum" for the real ones!

❑ Look sharp, big smiles, and do NOT spend a penny on anything that isn't needed at home or office.

❑ Remember what Fred Barge says in his essential book titled: *Are You The Doctor, Doctor?*

"Once a chiropractor is seeing 35 visits a week, the doctor should never have to advertise again."
- Fred Barge DC

I was taught that at 100 visits a week, all paid advertising can be eliminated. A doctor should be able to completely self-generate and grow a practice from there. I personally now teach that at 200 visits a week a doctor should never have to pay for marketing again.

Always remember the simple formula...

RESULTS come from: Putting in the **Time**, the **Energy**, and the **Money**.

Little time + little energy + little money = Little practice.

Big Time + Big Effort + Big Money = BIG, happy, fun, profitable practice.

Our stats always reveal the EXACT amount and quality of effort we have put in to our practice.

Question: *Tory, why am I not getting many new patients?*

Answer: *You aren't doing anything to cause new ones to come in!*

We Will Always Get an Exact Return Based Perfectly on the Amount of Effort and Energy We Have Put in FIRST.

For Every <u>Action</u> There Is an Equal and Opposite <u>Reaction</u>.

A 2 effort gets you a 2 return. A 20 effort will always get you a 20 return. Never think a 2 effort will get you 20 return.

Important story:

A salesman back in the 1960s was driving down a dusty gravel road on a blistering hot August day in rural America. One farm after another he rolled along with no air conditioning. He suddenly came over a hill and saw a farm much different than the others. The house was painted a sharp white and the barns were a stunning red. The yard was deep green and mowed perfectly. There were beautiful flowers blooming, healthy cattle meandering about in one field, and well-manicured crops in another. *Wow, what a place this is!* He says to himself.

He then notices the farmer on a tractor out in the field so he pulls over near the fence line. The dust settles, he gets out, slams the heavy door shut and leans on the fence for a much-needed break.

The farmer sees him and rumbles over on his rough old tractor. Arriving with a puff of black smoke, he shuts the tractor down, takes his hat off, and with an incredibly weathered hand he wipes his brow. The skin on the back of his neck almost black from the dirt and years in the sun. His skin like old leather with deep creases that only decades of day after day work in the elements could create.

The salesman knew he was now in the presence of a serious man who had worked harder and for more years than anyone he had ever met before.

What can I do for you? Says the farmer in a slow deep voice looking down confidently from his seat.

My what a beautiful farm God has blessed you with! The salesman says warmly.

The farmer then replies: *Well not really, you should have seen this place when God had it all to himself.*

We Have Already Been Given Everything We Need!

We have eyes that can see, ears that can hear, hands that can work, feet that can walk, a mind that can learn, and a mouth that can speak. Not to mention a country that allows us to have our own business. We can totally control our own schedule and income. It is an incredible thing!

What you do with everything you have already been given is what makes a great life. There is never anyone or anything to blame.

I think it is funny when I hear people say things like: *I pray for God to help me this and help me that...*

God has already done His part by giving you everything and all the tools and opportunity you could ever need. Now, what are YOU going to do with it?

A favorite saying: *God helps those who help themselves.*

Affirmations Cause the Mind To Visualize:

We have many affirmations for many purposes. Here is an example of one. Good affirmations direct the mind and can completely change the course of your life. They certainly have for me!

My practice is growing! I am busy and getting busier! New and returning patients are calling and coming in every day! _____ patients per week is easy! The more patients I see the more fun I have! My patients refer others in for my care. I am the Family Wellness, Medicare, and Injury Care expert! New patients call and come in from multiple sources every day. My checking account always has a great surplus. Collections are easy! I expect lots of patients and I get lots of patients. I expect great collections so I get great collections. I attract patients, referrals, and money with ease. When the phone rings it brings good news and great wealth. My results are excellent with every patient. I tell more people every day how I can help them. I love what I do and do what I love. I do more therefore I get more. When in doubt I crank into action! I serve with love, gratitude, certainty, and presence. I am always thankful!

And one last time: **We love you and we can help you!**

MODULE 12 *Money Flow & the Business of Practice*

Prior to this book, I used to give out a very brief **Start-up Essentials** guide. I will include it here as review, and to give you a few more tips.

After this, I will have some key points on Money Flow and the Business of Practice.

Chiropractic Start-Up Essentials

--- THE CHIROPRACTIC PURPOSE ---

To attract and help as many people as possible with natural chiropractic care while building and maintaining a balanced and successful life.

--- READ THIS CAREFULLY ---

In creating a new chiropractic office, you will be creating an experience for your patients: What they see, hear, touch, and feel from the moment they walk in to the moment they leave on each and every visit. The experience you create and whether or not the patients like it is a critical determining factor in your success.

In other words: Create a place that people like, do something that people like, be someone that people like, hire staff that people like then add your excellent clinical and business skills and you WILL be successful.

--- NOW READ THIS ---

Starting and opening a chiropractic office is secondary to the fact that YOU ARE STARTING A BUSINESS. Chiropractic is simply the service you will be providing within it.

You must learn and know EVERYTHING possible about owning a successful business. You're responsible for EVERYTHING! You can never say *I don't know how to do that* or *I'm not very good at that*. You MUST figure it out quickly. If ever in doubt, call an expert.

It is 100% YOUR responsibility to know EVERYTHING about your business, EVERTHING connected to it, EVERY square inch of it, how EVERYTHING works and who to call for EVERYTHING.

--- AND READ THIS ---

Getting started in practice revolves around <u>one thing</u>: How much money can you get?

It takes money to start a business, usually double what you think. If you think it will take $50,000, plan on needing $100K.

Get money – get space – build space – get legal – systems in place – office done – open – serve – create profit – save – pay-off debt – get better – succeed!

MASTER CHECKLIST

❑ Graduate from Chiropractic College.

❑ Pass all State and National Boards.

❑ Get State license.

❑ Acquire start-up money from any source you can.

❑ Buy NOTHING without talking to your accountant and coach first.

❑ Sign NO leases without asking an attorney first.

❑ Collect and keep ALL business cards and contacts.

❑ Save <u>every</u> receipt for everything <u>forever</u>, labeled by year.

❑ Realize Sales and Use tax is due on items purchased out of state.

❑ Understand you will have Fed taxes, State taxes, Payroll taxes, Sales and Use taxes, and sometimes Provider taxes.

❑ Promote like you are out to save the world!

Key point:

Making big money is harder than you think because the system is set up to take more when you earn more. Non-business owners who are "employees" will never understand this. People who earn little want someone else to pay for everything. i.e. you via you paying more taxes so they can sit back and get more free stuff from the government.

It is smart to understand that those who don't work as hard, want those that do to give them more free stuff. This is just the way it is. Make money, save money, and don't tell people about it. Show it by having a great life!

❑ Know that insurance will be a big part of your life: Unemployment Insurance, Workers Comp Insurance, Business Insurance, Umbrella Insurance, Auto Insurance, Property Insurance, Health Insurance. Get a good local agent – they will be a referral source.

❑ Get it in your brain now: If you don't absolutely need it to see people – DON'T buy it. Goal is to get open with the least amount of money.

❑ Create name, get EIN, register name with Secretary of State.

❑ Put in calendar to renew your business every year with your state.

❑ Again: You will owe State, Federal, Provider, and Sales and Use tax in most states. Figure out what taxes you owe in your state.

❑ Find and secure your location, or buy a practice.

Key point:

Choose a location based on its ability to sustain your business long term. The "go where you like it" is more for where you live. Put your office in a location than enables you to see the most people, and earn the most.

This will make you happier than having an office in a dead zone simply because *you* like it there. It is about them... not you.

❑ Negotiate on any leases! Free months of rent, buildout allowance/ TI, lowers bumps each year.

❑ Open business checking account in business name.

❑ Get good phone number and fax/credit card line.

❑ Choose new professional e-mail and web address.

- [ ] Get NPI numbers, both personal and corporation.

- [ ] Question the value every expense.

- [ ] Get credentialed with Medicare and any other insurance companies.

- [ ] Study WINNERSEDGE Medicare material on our website.

- [ ] Let your State Board know your situation. Make sure your business is filed properly – they will explain this.

- [ ] Make sure Malpractice Insurance is in place: 2 Mil/4 Mil not 1/3.

- [ ] Have business insurance in place.

- [ ] Get umbrella policy.

- [ ] Create logo, order business cards and stationery. Do this right the first time – then it will be done forever.

Key point:

You are creating a brand. Your name, logo, sign, business card, colors, decals, website, everything matters and is important for your success long term and for the value of your practice.

Note: We recommend your legal name include your last name but the practice be named differently via a DBA. There are many reasons for this.

Example: Smith Chiropractic LLC DBA Surfside Health and Wellness Center.

- [ ] Initiate website creation. Reserve all relevant URLs. We have recommendations for this.

- [ ] Engineer floor plan. Get help with this and get it right the first time.

- [ ] Be money careful! When in doubt, ask your coach.

- [ ] Choose a contractor, but don't trust them too much.

- [ ] Initiate buildout, order signage, decals, carpet, etc.

- [ ] Order all equipment, copier, computers, software, desks, chairs.

- [ ] Acquire all supplies, forms, decorations, posters.

- [ ] Secure all billing elements, electronic biller, credit card terminal.

- ❏ Create all marketing pieces and have ready to go. Paper and mail.
- ❏ Secure screening locations and have ready to go.
- ❏ Simplify personal life and personal expenses to the extreme.
- ❏ Attend all WINNERS**EDGE** Seminars and Trainings. Experiences are what bring growth. You can't learn from experiences you are not having.
- ❏ Visit nice established offices to observe and note what you need.
- ❏ Monitor ALL elements of EVERY process. People will mess up.
- ❏ Remember things take time to get so order ASAP. X ray, tables, and anything custom.

Key point:

If you purchased a practice - good for you. Now it is time to bring it up to WINNERS**EDGE** speed.

This must be done systematically based on budget. Goal is to maintain volume and build from the existing patient base and patient list. There is a process for this.

- ❏ If you don't absolutely need it, DON'T get it!
- ❏ Keep at least $20K aside FIRST for promo and marketing.
- ❏ Remember in chiropractic, the best marketer wins. Again: You are a marketer of chiropractic first. A businessperson second, a DC third. Become a student of marketing and persuasion. Get and read *Selling The Invisible* by Beckwith. It will change your life forever! Stop and order it right now! Think about the title and how true it is.

Sometimes you will be distracted. He wants to play but Dad wants to read from the first chiropractic textbook ever written.

There are 16 hours in a day and 112 waking hours in every week. There is plenty of time to do everything you need to do, so you can then have fun doing the things you want to do.

- ❏ Did I mention that the best marketer is the one who has the busiest and most profitable practice?
- ❏ Be reading chiropractic books of all kinds to stay grounded and powerful.
- ❏ Study Consultation, Report, and ALL 5 Plays per the WE System.
- ❏ Get appointment book and schedules set for clinic and team.
- ❏ Have hours posted on the front door and everywhere online.
- ❏ Create Black Book with all goals/stats for next 3 years.
- ❏ Watch all WE training videos, some several times.
- ❏ Complete buildout.
- ❏ Get Certificate of Occupancy.
- ❏ Those who say things like "It is only $200 bucks" are those who run out of money.
- ❏ Get DC and CA command centers fully ready.
- ❏ Avoid all the sharks that want a piece of you now. Say NO. They will start calling and dropping in as soon as you open. Ad people, MRI people, you name it.
- ❏ Did I mention to not spend any money unless it is essential to get started?
- ❏ Dress like a WINNER from now on. You aren't a peasant student anymore. What you wear matters huge if you want to win.

Key point:

People hear with their eyes. People buy with their eyes. Look like someone they see as credible, smart, powerful, and capable.

Lose any self-centered *I'll wear whatever I want* mentality. Look like a PRO. What others think of you is FAR more important than what you like or don't like wearing.

**What you are speaks so loudly I can't
hear what you are saying.**
- Emerson

❑ Have all systems working and everything legal before opening. Just because equipment is in place does <u>not</u> necessarily mean you are ready to open.

❑ Start with a CA whenever possible. Follow the hiring procedure.

❑ Have payroll set up via WINNERSEDGE Protocol.

❑ Read and study all WINNERSEDGE Booklets.

❑ Complete all 20 WINNERSEDGE "Installations" <u>fully</u>!

❑ We recommend doing all billing in house. This is too important to trust any outside company to do. Billing must be mastered. The PRO chiropractor and team are all experts at this.

❑ Sample Promo Explosion. Two phases: One to get rolling and get the kinks worked out with systems and procedures, and the second to add momentum and gain popularity.

Phase I

- Create, print, and dish 1000 to 3000 WE NPGs.

- Intro letter and business card to ALL contacts, family, and friends. (This is why you save all business cards and contacts)

- Have website running nicely with a great offer.

- Goal is 100+ per week in under 90 days.

Phase II

- Paper and direct mail promo sent out.

- Facebook Ad starts.

- Telemarketing blitz.

- Engage in company talks.

- Weekly screenings.

- After 100 a week is reached, paid marketing may not be necessary if your office runs properly and you are well scripted.

❑ We have contacts for all marketing angles. It is simply a matter of how fast you want to grow and what your budget will allow.

Key points:

- Create your Curriculum Vitae (CV). It is a fancy name for the resume of a professional person. You will be asked for your CV many times. Use mine as an example for formatting.

- Understand how much your OVERHEAD really is.

- Operate and grow with FEARLESSNESS.

- Everything must be a SYSTEM.

- You are a marketer – a chiropractor – and a business owner. The business owner part is commonly the one that usually makes or breaks the DC. Decide now to become an expert not only in chiropractic but also in the business of chiropractic!

- Always be aware of the LANDMINES and avoid distractions or anything that might get you off mission.

- MISSION and VISION. *What are you trying to build?*

- What will your office look like when complete and running perfectly?

- ULTIMATE GOALS. What do you really want in your Love, Health, Career, and Money life? I mean really want?

- Be RELIABLE. This means you are always on time and never need to be reminded.

- Be tough and have DURABILITY. This means that you are tough and can make it through the good and the tougher times in life without falling apart.

- Practice is a MARATHON. Good systems will get you there a winner. There are no schemes to *make it big* so you can then kick back. Being smart and steady is what wins in chiropractic!

- LOVE heals everything. There is equal good and bad in everything. When you finally see this truth - you are left with only love.

- ONEMANSHIP. You must know how to do everything in your practice and business life, from touching up the paint, to handling insurance, to managing people, to paying the bills, to being the doctor!

- Have a COACH. The top DCs get there and stay there with coaching. No fumbling on your own. We never wait to WIN!

Become famous for results, famous for service, and famous for being the best chiropractor who ever lived in your area!

The information offered here represents the opinion of the author. For all business decisions check with the appropriate attorney, accountant, or other professional. It is 100% your responsibility to adhere to any federal, state, or local laws and State Chiropractic Board rules. Because someone else is doing it means nothing. You alone are responsible for all your decisions and actions.

Check this out:

Modernized Chiropractic. The first chiropractic textbook in 1900! By Smith, Langworthy and the amazing Minora Paxson DC.

Money Flow and the Business of Practice!

My accountant handles chiropractors exclusively and his father did for many years before him. He is at the core of my success team and at the core of the WINNERSEDGE success team.

He and I recorded a two-hour video for my clients. I have wanted a video like this for 22 years now. If a chiropractor is able to start with this information there is no doubt they can be millions farther ahead down the road. I know I would have been! Here are the basic points from *The* WINNERSEDGE *Chiro Business and Accounting Bootcamp.*

Entity Selection:

- Corporation.

- S Corporation.

- Partnership.

- Single Member LLC.

- Each will have specific filing, recording, recordkeeping, and documentation requirements, depending on the classification you have chosen.

- Nearly all chiropractors are S Corporations or Single Member LLCs. If you are considering a multi-doctor clinic you will almost certainly be an S Corporation.

- The only difference between the two is how income is taxed. An S Corp has a different tax amount for profit and payroll. An LLC has the same tax amount across the board. The money flow processes are exactly the same.

Selecting a Bank for Your Business Needs:

- There are benefits of small banks or credit unions rather than larger national banks. With online banking there is almost no benefit to being with a large bank these days. Consider a small local bank or credit union near your office.

- They commonly have lower fees.

- Lending decisions are made locally.

- Tend to be more personable so that you can build a relationship with them vs. be just another anonymous person.

- All you need is a simple business checking account with its corresponding business debit and one business credit card.

- You also need a simple personal checking account with its corresponding personal debit and one personal credit card.

- Another savings or "wealth" account can also be started here.

- Simplicity is very powerful. You do not want credit cards from all over the place and multiple banks for business and personal checking accounts.

Business Credit Card:

- You should have a business credit card with your name and your business name below your name.

- Goal is to only have one business credit card and one personal credit card and no other credit cards of any kind. No store cards.

- Business credit cards are for legit business expenses ONLY.

- NO EXCEPTIONS!

- What is in your clinic checking account is NOT your money. It is the business's money.

- What you collect is NOT your income. It is the business's income. Chiropractors make the epic error of saying they make $50,000 a month because their clinic collects $50,000 per month. WRONG. You "make" what you get after all expenses and taxes are paid. Which, in this case, is more like $12,000 per month.

- The business has a Tax ID number or an Employer Identification Number which is essentially a Social Security number for a business. You are simply trusted to handle it. Once tax has been paid and the money is in your personal account you can then do whatever you want.

3rd Party Payments:

- Venmo, Zelle, Square Cash, GoFundMe.

- These are NEVER for business purposes. Do not pay from them or receive money from them ever for your business.
- NO EXCEPTIONS!
- These are personal tools or apps to send and receive money.
- They are great but use them for personal transactions only.

Payroll Payments to Employees:

- All employees complete a W4 and required information for employment and payroll.
  - FYI: Claiming 0 (zero) on a W4 deducts the most money and assures a tax return.
- We recommend you have an accountant who can do all the books, payroll and accounting.
- This is much better than having one person bookkeeping, another company doing payroll, then somewhere else an accountant trying to piece it all together.
- Remember the key lesson from *The Science of Getting Rich:*

  It is not really the number of things you do, but the EFFICIENCY of each separate action that counts.
  - Wallace Wattles 1912

- The following must all be run through payroll:
  - Hourly pay
  - Commissions
  - Bonuses
  - Birthdays, awards, length of service
  - Seminars, trainings, events
- We never recommend a salary for any employee.
- All hours are added up and submitted. Any over 40 in a week are paid at time and a half. Time to and from any work is not paid.
- Bonuses get added on. An example of a pay submission for a person getting paid every two weeks: 80 regular, 6 time and a half plus bonus of $250.

- Never just write a check to an employee. If it does happen, make sure the appropriate tax is withheld. (I know a DC in prison right now for two years because he did not pay the payroll tax for his employees.)

- All payroll should be done via direct deposit.

- NEVER take cash out of a business account to give to an employee or for any other reason. No using a business credit or debit card at an ATM ever. The second you do you will personally owe tax on that money.

Knowledge is Power:

A DC asks you: *I am just not getting many people to come in, what do I need to do?*

Your answer?

My answer: *Well doctor, I have a few questions for you:*

> *What is chiropractic?*
> *How does chiropractic work?*
> *What is subluxation?*
> *What does an adjustment do?*
> *When will your care make my X-ray straight?*
> *What makes the crunching sound?*
> *Why doesn't it just stay better?*
> *When will the pad grow back from you working on me?*
> *What if a patient asks you if chiro care causes strokes?*
> *How is chiropractic different from physical therapy?*
> *Does exercise do the same thing as chiropractic?*
> *Why don't I just get a massage instead?*

I have never seen a new grad be able answer these well enough for patients to be convinced. Your knowledge of the common questions and your ability to answer them without even blinking or looking away is what will make or break you.

Many DCs are faking their way. They don't really know the answers to these. And where would they ever learn them?

Hang with us and you will know <u>exactly what to say</u> in every situation!

What Is A Deductible Business Expense?

- A "write off" or deductible expense is money spent by the business that the IRS has determined can be deducted from the amount of money you pay taxes on.

- You want to collect and deposit ALL money into the practice checking account. All expenses are paid from this single business account.

- Expenses required to operate the business plus staff payroll is commonly called your "overhead."

- Once all business expenses including staff payroll are paid, this leaves gross profit.

- Gross profit is the amount you owe tax on.

  Example:

Total collections for the month	$72,000
Total expenses and payroll.	- $42,000
Gross profit	$30,000
Tax due for the month	- $14,000
Net profit	$16,000

- Net profit = What you earned = Your money.

- Taxes are a LOT more than any new graduate realizes. Those who have a job and see taxes come off their paycheck think taxes are high. That is only because they don't own a business.

  Once you own a business you will see taxes take on an entirely new meaning.

- You CANNOT pay from the business account (even if you are with business related people) any entertainment like golfing, social events, shows, or sporting event tickets.

- 50% of meals can be deducted if you keep the complete receipt. Write on it who all was there and what the meeting was for.

- You CANNOT pay from the business checking account any gym memberships, golf memberships, or club memberships.

- Only chiropractic associations, Rotary club, or similar can be paid from the business.

- Paid through the business, ran through the business, deducted, expensed, and "written off" all basically mean the same thing.

- Donating money to a legit charity or 501c organization can be paid through the business and is deductible. We recommend all giving come from the business account.

- GoFundMe donations are NOT deductible and should never be paid through the business. GoFundMe is a place where people donate to other people, not from businesses to people.

- It is fine to donate to GoFundMe but do it from your personal account. If you use your business account it will be considered income to you, which will be taxed. This means it will cost you a lot more to make this donation than you thought.

  Example: You make a mistake and donate $500 from your clinic account to a GoFundMe. Your accountant properly classifies this as income to you and not a deductible expense. This causes you to owe $400 more in tax. Why $400 more?

  Also, how much do you have to collect to donate $500 to a GoFundMe?

Answer:		
	Collect	$1800
	Overhead	- $ 900
	Gross profit	$ 900
	Tax	- $ 400
	Net profit to donate	$ 500

- Legit marketing expenses are deductible. Wearing a clinic T-shirt to the gym does not make the gym membership deductible.

- Putting a clinic logo decal on your car or truck does not make any of your vehicle expenses deductible.

- If you get the gym owner to allow you to have a banner in their gym at a cost of $150 per month, this is deductible as the IRS can walk in and see the banner. Having a few business cards sitting up at the gym counter is NOT the same.

Paying Yourself as An S Corp Owner:

- A "draw" or "distribution" is when you move money from your business account into your personal account without running it through payroll to have all the taxes taken out.

  The tax is still due and will be accounted for when you make your weekly, monthly, or quarterly tax deposit.

- What makes an S Corp appealing to many is that you pay tax on your paycheck from the clinic. You then pay a lesser amount of tax on any additional profit from the business that you pay yourself via a draw.

- Payroll tax may be 39.5% and the tax on the profit may only be 20% for example.

- Some doctors think they can work the system. They take a small paycheck then the rest of their pay as a draw in order to take advantage of the lesser tax on the draw.

- The truth is the IRS demands that the ratio of payroll to draw be correct. They do not state a percentage but for our purposes here we recommend you pay yourself through payroll at least 70%. Then maybe the remaining 30% through a monthly draw.

- The mistake would be to pay yourself $1000 every week then at the end of the month take a $15,000 draw. Much better to have a weekly paycheck of $3000 and a monthly draw of $3000.

- Remember, there is no hiding from the IRS. They know your business 100 times better than you ever will.

It is kindergarten level auditing for them to uncover the path and destination of every single dollar coming into and out of your office.

Paying Yourself as a Single Member LLC:

- We recommend a weekly paycheck for all DCs in all situations.

- We recommend an automatic state and federal tax deposit also be made weekly.

- At the end of the month if there is additional profit you can take a draw if desired.

- All profit, regardless of how it gets into your personal account is, taxed the same.

- With the information given it seems a no brainer to be an S Corp because at least you can save a little on tax. But no, there are many other factors that only a qualified accountant can review to recommend the best entity for your situation.

How Should Cash Flow from a Business?

1. You pay business operating expenses required to keep the business open (rent, payroll, electricity, etc.).

2. Pay all business and equipment loans.

3. Pay all estimated tax payments.

4. Pay yourself based on your collections, tax structure and personal budgeting needs.

5. Your weekly after-tax paycheck should cover all your personal expenses every month.

   - Know what it costs you to live! (Most never do.)

   - If your living expenses, auto, student loans, plus everything else add up to $5000 per month. Then be sure to pay yourself enough to cover this.

     Very few doctors have their own payroll set up properly. From this error, all subsequent money flow then falters.

   - Seems obvious, but what happens is a doctor does not know what their monthly personal expenses really are. Their paycheck is not enough so they end up spending (stealing) business money for personal expenses.

     This is the nightmare you never want to get into. This money is considered a draw and is taxable, but the doctor did not account for it. They then owe unexpected additional tax.

     Doctors like this are always wondering why their taxes seem like they are a lot more than they should be.

     These doctors simply need to increase their paycheck and auto tax deposits to cover their personal life. And/or decrease their personal spending!

- It is fine to leave excess funds in the business checking account. It is a great feeling to be able to pay cash for unforeseen expenses and equipment upgrades.

Personal Draws and Distributions:

- Personal payments should NOT be paid from any business account including:
  - Home, home equity, car, boat, and any other personal loan payments.
  - Child's schooling tuition or meal payment plans.
  - Grocery and household bills.
  - Personal credit cards.
  - Personal utilities.
  - Personal life, home, car, or disability insurance.
  - Personal investment funding and non-qualified investments.
  - Deposits to personal savings or money market accounts.
- Limit yourself to a weekly paycheck and one draw per month.
- Student loans must be paid from your personal account.
- NO EXCEPTIONS!

Crushing Student Loan Debt:

- Loan consolidation may be good, it may not be. Talk to me before doing this.
- Forbearance or deferment of loans is horrible. Never do this.
- Income based repayment is a trap. Never do this if possible.
- You must pay at least the interest every month plus a little towards principal.
- Find out how much the interest is every month, break it down to the day. You must be paying at least this much.
- I have seen doctors call me for help who owe $360,000 in student loans because they were asleep at the wheel.

- Confront all money situations head on. There is no hiding from what you owe. Boldly lay it all out on the table.

My *Practice Growth and Money Flow Online Bootcamp* is specifically designed to assess your entire financial situation and the plan to create money velocity! This training literally changes the entire financial future of our members overnight.

Personal Vehicle Use for Business:

- Traveling to and from work is not a business deduction.
- Purchasing a vehicle in the business name is never recommended.
  - A vehicle is not considered essential, customary, or ordinary to a chiropractic practice.
  - Insurance and interest on vehicle loans is more expensive if under a business name.
  - Vehicles can expose your entire business to litigation in the event of any injury or accident. Do you want attorneys coming after you AND your business if you cause an accident?
- Business deductions can be achieved by tracking your business related travel.
  - Use the MileIQ App to track personal and business drives.
  - To deduct a drive, you must have a legit business purpose for the miles driven like continuing education, seminars, hauling equipment, or home visits. Going to the chiropractor, or to visit chiropractor friends does not count.
  - There is not much to save here. Track your drives but as a rule consider all vehicle expenses as personal.

What Insurances Are Important to Have in Place?

Chiropractors getting started in practice have no idea what insurances they must have. Insurance is no place to try and save money. Not having the correct insurance in place if an incident occurs can be catastrophic financially.

160

All business-related insurance is tax deductible and can be paid from your clinic account. Never pay for personal insurance policies from the business account. If you do this it represents poor money management and is considered income to you and will be taxable.

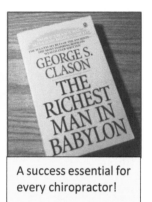

A success essential for every chiropractor!

With the exception of my malpractice policy, I have every insurance policy with one agent and one company. I seek simplicity and to get a volume discount. It is amazing how fast they handle things for me when I need them. There is no doubt they value me as a good customer.

Number one on nearly every experts list of books to read about handling money is: *The Richest Man in Babylon* by George Clason. In it he reveals The Laws of Gold. One of them is:

Guard thy treasures from loss.

- Arkad

Malpractice Insurance:

- You must have this in place before you adjust anyone. We recommend having a $2,000,000/$4,000,000 occurrence policy that has administrative hearing coverage. It is worth the small extra cost to have this additional coverage.

- Most doctors don't know this, but your malpractice policy only covers you in the state you practice. It is incredibly risky to ever adjust anyone outside your home state.

- Picture all the chiropractors adjusting each other at events all over the country. Only the ones in their home state are covered in case a rare adverse event were to occur.

Business Insurance Policy:

- Insurance to cover everything inside the clinic. The landlord will have a policy to cover everything beyond the walls.

- This must be enough to replace everything in the clinic if a total loss were to occur.

Workers Compensation Insurance:

- Once you have any employees you will have a Workers Comp policy in case any employee gets hurt at work. It is very rare that it will be needed, but we must have it in place just the same.

- The premium here will be based on what your payroll is. To determine this, they will often audit your payroll to see if their premium for the policy is correct.

- Observe that hiring another employee silently raises your overhead a little as your UI premium increases with each one.

Unemployment Insurance (UI):

- This will automatically be paid by your accountant or payroll company. Money here goes into a fund so if a person is terminated they can file for unemployment benefits.

- Many doctors think that if an employee leaves and files for unemployment it will cost them money. It does not, the UI policy pays the former employee, not you.

- I have never seen UI costs go up by any measurable amount if you have an occasional employee file for UI benefits.

- If an employee leaves and wants to collect any earned unemployment benefits, great, that is what it is there for.

- You do not seek to buy this policy, it is automatically in your accounting just like the Social Security deduction.

Employment Practices Liability Coverage (EPLI):

- Coverage for alleged wrongful employment practices. Claims by employees against an employer such as discrimination, harassment, and wrongful termination.

- This is an extra policy to cover if an employee sues you. No matter how wrong it may seem, or how frivolous the assertions are, employees are protected by the government. Sometimes overprotected.

  Example: You fire an employee. They were late all the time, texting while at work, and failed to learn how to communicate properly with patients. Several patients have complained about them and they stink up the reception room every time they go to the bathroom.

Totally unbeknown to you, they get mad and instead of seeking to learn and improve the real problem which is themselves, they feel entitled and direct their anger towards you.

They hire a money seeking attorney and sue you, creating a narrative that you were sexist, unreasonable, that you didn't pay them properly, and that you said things that made them feel uncomfortable (like that they need to show up to work on time).

You then get a scary letter in the mail from their attorney accusing you of all this. It includes some insane demand for money. You become furious. This forces you to hire an attorney for $350 an hour. The legal bills start to add up and amount to a few thousand dollars per month.

They have no real case and no proof of anything. You were totally right to let the person go, but the lawyers will go back and forth and cost you tens of thousands in the process.

Your attorney tells you to just settle for $30,000 otherwise the mess will go on for a couple years costing you much more. It is called "legal extortion" and happens every day in every city in America. No matter how wrong it is, there is nothing you can ever do to change it.

- Almost nobody even knows Employment Practice Liability Coverage exists! Have this in place and sleep better at night.

Disability Insurance:

- This is a hot topic. If you are unable to practice for any reason you can get up to around $7000 per month depending on your policy limits.

- These policies are expensive. They are around $4000 a year for any real benefits. Because of this, many newer doctors don't get it. Yet they are the ones who need it the most because if you cannot work and your income stops, not having a policy in place can be devastating financially and emotionally.

- We have ways to keep a practice rolling in the event of a doctor not being able to practice, but we do recommend you look into having a disability policy in place.

- Doctors with a lot of money saved, which they can live on in case of an emergency, may not need a disability policy. I have one anyway. Insurance is very inexpensive compared to the benefits you get should you need it!

- Disability insurance must be paid personally and <u>not</u> from the business. This is <u>you</u> personally buying a policy to protect <u>your</u> personal income in the event you are injured. It has nothing to do with your business.

Auto Insurance:

- Obviously have auto insurance in place. I recommend $1000 deductibles on comp and collision. You can decide what you want. No deductible is nice but it does cost a bit more.

- In many states if you own more than one vehicle you can "stack" coverage. For example, right now I have 5 cars and have chosen to "stack" the coverages. Instead of just the normal $20,000 in medical benefits available in my state, I would get $100,000 if an incident occurred.

- All auto insurance is paid by you personally and never from the business.

Homeowners Insurance:

- Smart to have for countless reasons. Visit with your agent and be sure you have enough.

- Critical to have on any rental properties you may own as well.

Renters Insurance:

- If you are renting this covers all your personal property. The landlord should have a homeowner's policy in place as well.

- Only an insurance expert can determine which policy is engaged depending on an event that occurs. Be sure to have yours in place!

Boat, Snowmobile, Jet Ski, RV Insurance:

- All toys need insurance. Imagine how many injuries occur with recreational toys and how underinsured many people find themselves. There is major risk here. Someone slips on your boat, a snowmobile crash injures someone, or a friend runs your Jet Ski into a dock, on and on. You need to understand what a policy on any toy will or will not cover.

- This is why you need an umbrella policy. It will cover whatever these small policies won't, up to the limit you purchase.

- Also know, as a chiropractor, people who have been injured on toys like this will come in as patients. These cases do not work like typical personal injury cases do. The coverage is much different.

I have an offshore powerboat that I love ripping around in. You can bet it is fully insured and I have an umbrella policy in place should anything ever happen to anyone I may take out boating. Be smart and be fully insured at all times.

If a person crashes a motorcycle, rarely do they have any medical benefits if they are injured. The coverage is primarily designed to cover anyone the driver injures and is liable for. This is why it is called "liability" coverage.

Personal Umbrella Policy:

- Like the name implies, this policy is there to cover anything that happens in your world that is beyond the limits of the first policy in place. It is not expensive to get $1,000,000 or more in additional coverage. Always have an umbrella policy.

- A person in a freak accident gets severely injured in your backyard and needs $300,000 of medical care and files suit for $500,000. If your homeowner's policy only covers up to $250,000 you better have an umbrella policy in place.

- Just imagine all the totally unpredictable things that happen in our country. Some are truly accidents and others are crazy things that somebody may want to sue you for. As a doctor you are a target and always will be. Be smart and have plenty of good insurance in place at all times.

Insurance for Any Valuable Items Like Jewelry:

- If you buy anything of value call your agent and see if it is worth insuring.

  Example: After 20 years of dedicated chiropractic practice you reward yourself with a $20,000 watch. Get it insured as well as any diamond rings or fine artwork. Insure anything of value you would want covered if it were stolen or damaged.

What Taxes Do We Have To Be Ready For:

It may seem like some of this material is boring. Talking about taxes and insurance may not be as exciting as your awesome new business card design but... if you ever want to be even a little wealthy, it is the boring material that you have to be really good at!

This is a lesson for life. Get good at the mundane and boring tasks since they are the foundation for all success in business. In football, for example, the team that blocks and tackles best is usually the team that wins the game, but how many kids are excited to practice blocking?

Federal Tax / IRS:

- You will owe federal tax on any profit the business makes. We recommend this tax deposit be automated and paid every week.

- The WINNER**SEDGE** *Small Amounts Weekly* concept for taxes, debts payments, and saving is one of many reasons our doctors are so successful.

State Tax:

- If your state has a state tax we recommend this also be paid weekly along with the federal.

Payroll Tax:

- This is the tax you must submit on behalf of your employees and yourself as an employee of the business.

- Your responsibility as an employer is to make sure all taxes are paid for all employees. This is another reason why we recommend your accountant handle all business payroll.

- Included in all this is the unemployment insurance and FICA, or Social Security. Your accountant will make sure the right amounts get to the right place.

Provider Tax:

- You may not believe this but in some states if you are a doctor you have to pay an additional tax.

- Here in the State of Minnesota doctors have to pay 2% of our total yearly collections, excluding Medicare or Medicaid, as an additional tax on top of all the others!

  We end up paying thousands more in tax every year simply because of the profession we chose.

  This motivates me to be even more successful. We still have the best country in the world to be successful. There is plenty of room for those who know how to work hard to create an incredible life!

Sales and Use Tax:

- This may be the least understood and most commonly mishandled tax of all. If you sell any products in your office you need to add the sales tax, then send the sales tax to your state.

  You can make these tax payments monthly, quarterly, or yearly depending on how much your sales are.

- If you buy anything out of state and that business does not charge you sales tax on the purchase and you use the items in your home state, you now owe what is called Use Tax on those items.

  Example: You buy a case of ice packs from a business in another state. They cost $120. You pay $120 plus $15 to ship them for a total charge on your card of $135. No problem, right? Wrong. No sales tax was paid, so you now owe the sales tax for these on your Sales and Use Tax Return!

- Sales and Use Tax return audits are one of the most common audits today. I have been audited for this.

  Example: An auditor from the State Department of Revenue came in to my office for three days and went through <u>every single receipt for every single thing</u> for the last three years. He put it all into a massive spreadsheet and said I owed $16,000 in unpaid Sales and Use Tax!

  I was able to provide proof that tax was paid for most of the items in question. I ended up owing $4000. It is easy money for them since practically no small business owners know about this or handle it right, including me at the time.

  From then on, I have been on top of this perfectly. I recommend you do the same.

- Be sure to file a Sales and Use Tax Return at the end of the year. Find out when this is due in your state. If you are selling quite a bit, or buying a lot from out of state, we recommend monthly Sales and Use Tax deposits.

Filing an Extension:

- Federal Tax Returns are due April 15th of each year. An extension can be filed if needed. Filing an extension can bring additional fees and late charges.

- If I hear a chiropractor say they had to file an extension, I know I am talking to a chiropractor who is in a financial mess.

- You should <u>never</u> have to file an extension. It is a sign of very upside-down money handling.

- Everybody in America knows their taxes are due April 15th. If a doctor still cannot get their taxes done on time and needs to file an extension, we have work to do to correct the doctor's money flow system.

- I estimate that less than 10% of chiropractors have a money flow system in place that is effective and promotes future wealth.

- There are many causes for this error. One is that the doctor is spending all their money out of order. They are likely spending money on themselves first, then on the practice, and then taxes last. A total money flow disaster.

- We should always pay taxes BEFORE we ever pay ourselves so we are NEVER behind. As I sit here my taxes are current to the week. I have not missed a weekly tax payment in years.

- The **WINNERSEDGE** Money Flow System for chiropractors is one of the smartest and most life changing developments in the history of the profession. You cannot retire on patient visits. You will need a lot of money saved. Set a goal to have at least $2,000,000.

Now realize -

If you were to analyze what appear to be the most successful chiropractors you know, you might quickly discover money flow problems, tax paying issues, disorganization, and costly inefficiencies.

What you see on the outside is a small part of the story. Many students and newer DCs will visit chiropractic offices and look at the space, the layout, furnishings, equipment, and colors when they should be looking at the goal and stat sheets, tax returns, donation amounts, weekly saving amounts, net worth, and all underlying money flow systems.

What is TRUE CHIRO SUCCESS?

At **WINNERSEDGE** I have coined the phrase **True Chiro Success.** My entire line of audio material is called the **True Chiro Success** audio series. Our seminar series is called the **True Chiro Success** seminar.

True Chiro Success means exactly what you think. The doctor enjoys honest and loving relationships. The doctor is well-conditioned mentally and physically. The doctor has their practice in wonderful order. The doctor is an excellent money manager on their way to significant wealth. Is this what you want? *To get this you must hang around this!*

What is True Chiro Success? Example 1

You pull up to visit a DC you hear is really "cranking" in practice. As you are walking in you notice a brand new Mercedes in the parking lot with a license plate that says: DCSRULE. *"That must be his car"* you say as you walk in.

"Wow what a nice office" you think as you enter. The place is really nice. Plus, the location is in the busiest retail strip mall in town.

You meet three CAs then the doctor. He is dressed really nice. You watch him see a few patients and visit a bit. You discover he is seeing 300 patients a week and collecting around $70,000 every month. He has the latest X-ray, therapy machines, and very nice treatment tables. You are impressed, this is the coolest office and most successful doctor you have ever met!

Now imagine

He and all his staff leave and you are allowed to snoop around in all drawers and computer files. You uncover he is $14,000 behind on last year's taxes. The car is leased for $1200 per month. His payroll is over $8500 every month.

Rent for this popular location is $4200 a month. He is not saving any money that you can tell, and not donating any money to those in need.

There are emails from his accountant saying he needs to stop spending and get his taxes current, and that he is also behind $40,000 for this year.

A young DC with a new and expensive vehicle is a classic sign that the doctor is trying to "look rich." But in reality, is likely a very poor money manager. Smart people are never fooled. We have a specific auto purchasing process for our clients who would much rather "be rich!"

You then open a folder and see he has three credit cards all with balances over $20,000. You open another file and see that even though he is 9 years in practice he still owes $187,000 on his student loans. You are shocked! *"Geez, what a mess"* you say to yourself.

Then it hits you that this guy just "looks rich" but has no money. Every penny that comes in to his practice goes right back out for personal extravagances, bills, and debt payments. You realize that in no way can he afford that car. His entire money flow is totally backwards. All the "invisible" things Tory talks about are a mess in this guy's life!

True Chiro Success means you have all the critical yet <u>invisible</u> systems in place. All banking, money flow, accounting, payroll, giving, money saving, and taxes are in beautiful, current, flowing order.

Notice I said <u>invisible</u>. In Jiu Jitsu we have a term called invisible Jiu Jitsu. This refers to all the things going on in a match that you <u>cannot see</u>. You cannot see pressure, or how heavy someone feels. You cannot see how strong a grip is. You cannot see weight distribution or fatigue, yet all these things are controlling your success in the match.

The same is true in practice. It is all the invisible things you cannot readily see that control your success.

Invisible Things You Cannot Easily See in a Chiropractor's Office:

- How much debt vs. how many assets does a doctor have?
- How much is the doctor giving away every month?
- Has the doctor established the habit of saving?
- Do they pay all their bills on time?
- Do people like to work with them or do they despise it?
- How financially organized is the doctor at their desk and online?
- How refined is the doctor's online bill pay?
- How much equity (or lack of) do they have in what they own?
- Does the doctor have clear, accurate, and written down goals?
- What is the doctor's net worth right now?
- Is the doctor's net worth growing or decreasing?

A Word About Net Worth:

Net Worth is your financial grade as a human being. Your money managing grade. It is <u>not</u> your grade as a person, but as a money handler.

Income and money habits are important. The primary and revealing way to measure this is with net worth.

What you <u>Own</u> – What you <u>Owe</u> = Net Worth

What is True Chiro Success? Example 2

You visit another chiropractic office. There is a very clean but several year-old Nissan Maxima sitting in the parking lot. You figure it must be her car. You walk in and notice the office is nothing fancy but it is nice and clean. One very well-trained CA introduces herself and takes you back to meet the doctor.

The doctor is dressed well and tells you she sees 200 visits a week and is collecting $40,000 per month. You visit for about an hour then leave thinking she was nice. You feel her practice was "ok" but nothing to brag about. It was nothing like the last office you visited.

Now imagine

You also get to snoop around her office. You notice her goals and stats are neatly on her desk. On the computer you see an email from her accountant congratulating her on paying off all her loans early, and how awesome it must feel to have her practice, car, and all student loans completely paid.

You then see on her desk a *Thank You card* from a charity she donates to every month. You open a drawer and find a bank statement showing she has $57,000 saved. "*Whoa this gal really has it together*" you say to yourself. You also see her work schedule is just 3 ½ days a week while the other guy was working 6 days a week.

Upon leaving, on the wall you see her in a really cool group picture that says WINNERSEDGE **DC BOOTCAMP.** "*Wow that looks like fun*" you think to yourself as you find yourself humbled by how wrong you were about her.

The Tortoise Beats the Hare is such a wise saying. Those with smart systems and habits over weeks, months, and years will end up super successful while others never will. This is what works for us. In fact, it is the ONLY way. **Grow practice + Pay debt + Auto save = $ Success.** It just takes some training to learn how to do it.

She actually IS rich and on her way to wealth. The DC you "thought" was rich has nothing but bills and stress.

In fact, you learn the other DC has a Net Worth of -$324,000 and this DC has a Net Worth of +$182,000. She is over $500,000 richer, yet the guy in the Mercedes makes fun of her for not being as busy in practice as he is!

Healthy and wealthy people love her. They can see in <u>her</u> the habits and self-disciplines that made her so successful. You drive away with a whole new perspective of what success <u>really</u> is.

Below is the **Chiropractor Power Index**. It quantifies the current level of power, awareness, discipline, self-honesty, effort, commitment, plus ability to solve problems and create success from a low of 7 up to a superior rating of 35. These criteria do not reveal everything about a person, but they accurately quantify who and what a person is right now as a chiropractor. A DC must score at least 22 on the **Power Index** to be considered for **GUARDIAN** status in the WINNERSEDGE chiropractic success group.

Mark the number 1 thru 5 that most accurately describes the DC

VOLUME   1 --------- 2 --------- 3 --------- 4 --------- 5

| 100 a wk. | 150 a wk. | 200 a wk. | 300 a wk. | 400+ a wk. |

COLLECTIONS   1 --------- 2 --------- 3 --------- 4 --------- 5

| Under $20k mo. | $20-40k mo. | $40-70k mo. | $70-100k mo. | $100k+ mo. |

CONDITIONING   1 --------- 2 --------- 3 --------- 4 --------- 5

50lb+ over weight	Not good	Ok shape	Good shape	Competition level
Excuses & lies rampant	Overweight	Can run a mile	Can run a 5k+	Marathon
No value for body	Still lying, in denial	Can do 1 pull-up	Several pull ups	10+ Pull ups
Clueless to the truth	Still overeating	Better Fueling	Eats better, Juices	Serious fueling

IMAGE   1 --------- 2 --------- 3 --------- 4 --------- 5

Never looks good	Looks OK sometimes	Decent dresser	Well put together	Very sharp always
Off weight & sloppy	Neglect still evident	Average image	More powerful	Serious charisma
No or frumpy suit	Suit looks cheap	Suit average	Sharp suit	Wow all the time
Unaware they smell	Still smells often	Ok hygiene	Good hygiene	Smells good

MONEY SKILL   1 --------- 2 --------- 3 --------- 4 --------- 5

| Behind, no system | Some systems in | Systems ok | Systems rolling | Money master |
| Debt dominates | Above water | Savings in place | $500k+ saved | Millionaire + |

INFLUENCE   1 --------- 2 --------- 3 --------- 4 --------- 5

Almost none	Some locally	More popular	Knows everyone	Everyone knows you
No power to refer	Attempts to	Rare referral	Has influence	People do what you say
Repels patients & others	No real power	Power with few	Power with many	People follow you
Almost nobody listens	Few listen	Close people listen	Many listen	People pay to listen

ENERGY   1 --------- 2 --------- 3 --------- 4 --------- 5
and
DRIVE

Weak	When convenient	Some energy	An achiever	A force to reckon with
Does nothing	Worry and doubt	Gets some done	Gets a lot done	Does it all and more
Excuses rampant	Breaks easily	Confidence emerging	Certainty	Utterly fearless

Add up all 7 numbers = [   ] Power Index

7 – 13   New or struggling person. Requires extensive, dedicated personal and professional training.
14 – 19   Some effort showing. A growing or possibly flatlined person. Must step up all training to grow.
20 – 25   A successful person. Needs continued training, mind work, conditioning and discipline.
26 – 30   A highly successful person who still has room to grow. Needs smart coaching and Mastermind group.
31 – 35   A Powerhouse ready for lifestyle design. Energy efficiency, Mastermind, and humility are critical.

In school we focus primarily on class, technique, exams, national boards, socializing, and graduation.

To be successful in practice there are an incredible array of new skills that we must develop and become proficient at.

Plan to Be or Become Great At:

- Explaining chiropractic to strangers, patients, and new employees.
- Speaking to small groups of adults, kids, and very smart people.
- Interviewing, hiring, employing, managing, and firing employees.
- Marketing, promoting, and selling chiropractic and yourself.
- Billing expertise and using the correct ICD-10 and CPT codes.
- Complying with your state chiropractic laws and board rules.
- Handling accounts receivable and accounts payable.
- Being an expert in managing and strategizing all business debts.
- Understanding leases and being a good tenant.
- Managing debit cards, credit cards, and all online banking.
- An expert with your payroll, accounting, and all taxes.
- An organized and religious saver and giver of money.
- A chiropractor with impressive office systems and scripting.
- All the clinical and technical expertise required with patients.
- A smart planner of the future for yourself and those around you.
- A design person, from business cards to flyers and everything else.
- Negotiation and persuasion skills with all types of people.
- Flat out selling people on trying chiropractic in your office.
- An image expert who is also very good at reading body language.
- A reader, seminar goer, and eternal learner.
- Managing and balancing time between practice and home.
- Cleaner, scrubber, and go-to repair person for the office.
- Financial planner and wealth creator for the future.
- A person who spends less than they make.
- A nice, likable, agreeable, and good person!

You must decide right now that you want to become great at EVERYTHING required in your practice.

Those that want to be the best in their profession are those who want to learn everything they can about it.

The Chiropractic Power Life is when a doctor fully embraces the chiropractic life of natural health and high-performance living.

It is a way of thinking and living that revolves around being great at everything you do!

There are basically four main areas of life: Love and Relationships, Health and Fitness, Career, and Money. Or: **Love, Health, Career and Money.** The DC living the Chiro Power Life wants to have all these in beautiful order!

The Chiropractic Power Life Includes:

Wonderful Relationships That Are Loving And Honest:

- We attract what we are. We choose who we date and marry. There is never anyone to blame. If you are happy – you chose them. If you are not happy - you chose them.

- Become the best version of yourself! Become successful in practice first, then you can attract the right person to you. There is no rush here.

Superior Health:

- The Chiro Power Life doctor is a serious mental and physical specimen. They don't have to tell anyone. People can already see that you are a person who takes their health seriously.

- This doctor uses a juicer, almost never has any caffeine or alcohol, and never takes any medication or drugs of any kind.

- Their kids have never had a vaccine or ever really been sick. Their home and lifestyle are a health seeking example of what chiropractic is and what chiropractic can do.

- They strive to lead a superior life 24 hours a day.

- They love and have conquered any bad programming from their past relating to health. They have good habits and they know it.

- Remember the great quote: *What you are speaks so loudly I can't hear what you are saying.* - Ralph Waldo Emerson

  A DC who is not living the Chiro Power Life, in no way can hide or try to talk past it. <u>You are what you are.</u> Everyone can see if you are the real thing or not. People buy what they see.

Advancing Career:

- The Power Life DC has their practice in perfect order. There is nothing left to do or fix. This doctor has no weak points in their office. They HAD weak points, but not any longer.

- They put in the time and do whatever it takes to create something impressive. Layout, systems, schedule, meetings, huddles, billing, treatment time, scripting, everything is on point.

- On coaching calls I ask these doctors if there are any practice issues we need to fix. They say: *Nope, everything is rolling great!*

Money Success:

- The Power Life DC has all the WINNER**SEDGE** practice systems and money flow architecture in place and working.

- They are giving, saving at least their age, debt is well under control, and the systems they have in place guarantee they will be a multi-millionaire come retirement time.

- To learn more about this you will want to get my *Money Chiropractic and You* book I referred to earlier.

The Chiropractic Power Life is when you have everything in your life in smart order. This requires an incredible amount of dedication, learning, and work to accomplish and maintain. It represents the ULTIMATE expression of the chiropractic man or woman!

It is also a good time to discuss what POWER is. <u>Power is your ability to make your life the way you want it.</u>

- Can you live in the house you really want to live in?

- Can you own the cars you really want to drive?

- Can you send your kids to the best schools in the area?

- Can you "save your age" every year or are you not able to? This means if you are 35 you are saving at least $35,000 a year.

- Can you buy any high quality organic food you like or do you have to be careful what you spend at the grocery store?

- Can you go anywhere in the world you want, anytime you want, or do you *wish* you could?

- Can you give an amount to charity that makes a big difference?

- Can you have whatever schedule you want every week?

- Can you buy and wear whatever clothes you want?

- Can you get yourself the best equipment for any hobbies you like?

- Can you do nice things for people when you want to, or do you say you *wish* you could help?

- If something lowers your income are you unaffected or do you get scared at any thought of your paycheck dropping?

Hang with me and you will become POWERFUL!

The number of doctors who truly have POWER is like 5%. This is the level you are shooting for.

Think about this again: *Power is your ability to make your life exactly the way you want it!* It is a main goal in life isn't it?

To develop power is FREE. Working hard, being on time, having integrity, having a gritty desire to win, reading, exercising, getting up early, being honest, caring about people, learning scripts, and managing time are all power-building qualities which are absolutely FREE!

Amazing, isn't it? We go to school, spend years and piles of money, yet all the things that will make a person really successful are FREE.

Those who develop power take this saying very seriously: *How you do anything, is how you do everything.* What does this mean?

Which reminds me of another favorite: *If you are too big for a small job, you are too small for big job.* To be successful in practice and develop POWER means taking pride in doing a million little things well.

How You Do <u>Anything</u> Is How You Do <u>Everything</u>!

Getting started in practice and all throughout your career there are countless landmines to be aware of and avoid.

There are many good reasons to join a success group like WINNER**SEDGE.**

One reason is so you can learn from the hundreds of years of experience of all the other doctors and CAs in the group. This arms you so you can avoid the landmines certain to cross your path in every phase of practice.

Another reason to join is so you can learn how to think, speak, and act in a way that will make you super successful as a chiropractor and as a person. Success in practice is learned. *Where are you going to learn it?*

Iron sharpens iron. There is no way an isolated doctor can ever do as well as a doctor who is continuously being motivated, challenged and pushed by other successful doctors from all over the country.

Hopefully you are dedicated enough to want to lead the Chiropractic Power Life!

Any discussion about avoiding the landmines in life must include the **3 Ds.** These are the MAJOR landmines to avoid. They require no explanation but I will say a few words anyway.

- **Debt:** Debt = Death. Mortgage = Death Pledge (Note <u>mort</u>uary and <u>mort</u>ician.)

  No more borrowing. Borrow only for a car or a house after graduation. A major principle we teach is that you <u>do not buy a house until your student loans are paid</u>. There are many reasons for this. Be happy renting until you can get the right house.

  I have consulted many doctors who have over 14 different debts. Your goal is to only owe on a house and a car. NO unsecured debt ever after your student loans are paid.

- **Divorce:** I had a great friend in college. He was from a wealthy family. He, his dad, and I were cruising in their boat one morning and out of nowhere his dad said: *You really want to have nothing someday? Go get yourself a divorce.* I never forgot that.

  This means if you get married, marry the right person. Everyone who gets divorced, back when they got married would have sworn they were marrying the right person.

  Here's some truth for you: We have been programmed to believe in love, fairy tales, Cinderella, Valentines Day, *a diamond is forever,* and other propaganda to make people believe love is something much different than what it really is.

  All love between adults is conditional. Repeat, all love between conscious adults is <u>conditional</u>. Conditions change in a relationship and the level of "love" changes with it, sometimes leading to failure of the relationship. This is much different from unconditional love. The love of a parent for a child or of a dog for their owner is more <u>unconditional</u>.

  You are considering enteing into a partnership with another human being for life. Better to be patient and <u>become self-actualized first</u>. This means you become successful and reach some goals first. Who you are as a student or as a new doctor is <u>nothing</u> like who you will be once you are established.

  Religion, family expectations, programming, and self-esteem (or lack of) all come in to play when considering marriage.

  My advice is: Think long term reality. Listen to your parents and siblings. Listen to the brutally honest opinions of your friends. (As well, give good honest opinions when you are asked.)

  And…become very successful FIRST. We attract what we ARE. If you become successful and winning in life, the caliber of people you attract will be very impressive!

  I wish you the best of success and happiness in this most challenging yet rewarding area of life.

- **Death** Take care of yourself. Be careful driving and <u>with everything you do</u>. Listen to your innate, expect the unexpected, and be around for a long healthy time!

Landmines You Are Likely to Face:

Landmines, errors, screw-ups, surprises, mistakes, plain ignorance, shortsightedness, bad luck, laziness, foolishness, intentional deceit, cheating, call them whatever you want.

An endless array of things will come at you as a chiropractor, as a business owner, and as a person. Our goal is to do everything so well and be able to think ahead such that nothing too bad ever happens. If by chance it does, we want to be prepared for it.

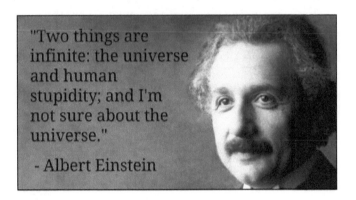

"Two things are infinite: the universe and human stupidity; and I'm not sure about the universe."

- Albert Einstein

Einstein is right and chiropractors are no exception. The array of goofy things I see doctors do is astonishing. So much so I recorded an audio set titled: *Chiropractic Fails, Foibles, and Foolishness!* I recommend you get it and all other WINNER**EDGE** audio and video materials. They each fill a key component of your practice success wheel.

Major Landmine Examples:

- You were lazy in school. You aren't a very good adjuster and you have not read, studied, or practiced what you were supposed to. You are also not very good at talking about chiropractic and persuading people to come and see you, so not very many do.

  You say that joining a coaching group is too expensive.

  After a few months of living off credit cards you can't pay your overhead. Instead of calling experts for help you just bail out of practice and get a job elsewhere. You blame the school. You blame chiropractic. Though there are successful chiropractors in every city, you still find a way to blame the "tough economy."

You say: *People just don't want to go to a chiropractor these days.*

You feel you wasted 4 years and $250,000, of which the loan payments are about to start and will NEVER go away. Not even a bankruptcy can make them go away.

- You open your new practice and think you have a great idea for a referral contest. Every person or business that refers a new patient gets a $20 Amazon gift card. It is going to be awesome! You tell everyone and even make a flyer that you give out around the area.

You start getting a few new patients and it seems to be working. You are off to a fine start. About 3 months later you get a letter from your State Board of Chiropractic Examiners. You say: *Huh, I wonder what this is for?* It is a complaint by another DC in your area who saw your referral contest flyer and turned you in.

You get in trouble for fee splitting and offering kickbacks. You have to pay a $15,000 fine. You get your license taken away for 6 months with 2 years of probation after that.

This is a total disaster! You think: *What am I supposed to do for 6 months?* Your wife is pregnant and you need every penny to keep this practice growing and survive at home.

You thought you were being nice to people with your great marketing idea. How nice is it now? And how do you tell all your current patients, friends and family you are out for 6 months?

This all could have been avoided if he would have read his state board rules for advertising. He could have been cranking, profitable, and with all systems safely in order happily awaiting the arrival of their first child.

- You wait until the end of the year to do your taxes and get surprised with a tax bill of $68,000. This buries you financially and takes 3 years with expert coaching to recover from. Just when you think you are all caught up you get a letter from the IRS saying you will be audited. You end up owing another $27,000. The intense financial stress almost ruins your marriage.

All this was easy to avoid if the doctor would have had the correct accounting and money flow system in the first place.

- You meet me while out with some other chiro friends. You have heard about me and make a point to say: *Good to meet you Tory, I am actually thinking of doing some consulting myself.* Knowing you are only a few years in practice I say: *Oh really?*

  You are a little arrogant and "think" you are smarter than the system. You go ahead and bill for a few services you didn't do, to the insurance companies you know will pay. You even send in a few visits for people that didn't come in that day. They are friends of yours so it will be okay. You figure nobody will notice.

  This is called insurance fraud. Secretly, investigators videotape and time everyone coming and going from your office via a van in your parking lot. Two investigators wearing hidden cameras and microphones pose as patients and record every word you say. They then monitor everything you bill.

  The Dept. of Commerce and police suddenly show up in the middle of a busy morning with lights flashing and raid your office. They take everyone's cellphone and all your computers. You have staff and patients literally wondering if they are on TV. Sure enough, your office makes the 6:00 news in a special segment called *Fraud Alert!*

  Now everyone in your town is talking about you and your mess. Your family, friends, patients, business connections, everyone.

  A one-year investigation concludes and you lose your license for 2 years, are fined $30,000 and have to pay back $152,000. You get sentenced to 24 months in prison for mail fraud and wire fraud.

- You want to be a big player in the PI game so you work hard to make the right connections. You decide to pay people to go out and get crash patients to come see you. When they come in you give the "runner" and the patient a cut of the collected money. Seems like a great plan. Everybody wins and is happy. You feel like a genius marketer that is out there "making it happen."

  At the bar you party it up and buy drinks for everyone since you are the high roller. Your other DC friends envy you for doing so much better than them in practice.

Either you have no idea or you simply don't care that everything you are doing is illegal. You certainly didn't read your state laws like Tory teaches.

You cannot use "runners" or "fee split" with anyone. Investigators show up, you lose your license, and have to pay back the $700,000 you collected from this over the last four years.

You get sentenced to prison for almost 3 years. How are you going to tell your 2-year-old and 5-year-old daughters that you won't see them for their next 3 birthdays or Christmas Holidays?

- You hear about "the WINNERSEDGE guy with the Dobermans from Minneapolis" who is supposed to be some chiro success expert. You call and are able to get in the group. You go back to your hometown where you know a ton of people. Tory teaches you the systems and he even designs your office. You are off to a great start and even have 100 new patients in one month!

With our systems and high performance coaching you are over 100 visits a day in under a year. The money is coming in so you ask: *Hey Tory, is it ok if I buy a new car and a new house?*

Tory says: *As long as all your student loans are paid, taxes are current, and you are auto saving your age then go ahead. But use the WE home and auto buying guidelines.*

You say: *Sounds good!* You excitedly go shopping for cars and a new house.

A couple years later you decide to do a Patient Appreciation Day. You put a flyer everywhere and advertise that the day is FREE for all patients. The day comes and you see 173 people and 23 new patients that day. Awesome!

But... Instead of it being free, you bill all 23 of the new patient's insurance companies for a Level 3 exam code 99203.

A patient sees this on a statement from her insurance company and turns you in. You get investigated. More billing errors are found.

You call me and I find out that you billed the new patients on a PAD, so in a serious coaching tone I ask: *Why in the world would you ever do that? WHAT WERE YOU THINKING?*

The State Board, the Attorney General, and the Department of Commerce all grill you asking: *Doctor Foolish, how can you do 23 Level 3 exams in one day when you see 173 people? The Code required 30+ minutes of face to face doctor time.* You have no answer.

Your license is revoked in your state. You now have no income but are ordered to pay back $220,000. You don't have the money, it was spent long ago.

Sure enough: *How you do anything is how you do everything.* It is discovered later that you lied and still owe over $176,000 on your student loans. In addition, instead of using the WE guidelines for buying a car and a home, you bought 3 brand new cars with monthly payments totaling over $2400 per month and a huge house with a payment of $4800 per month.

There you sit. No practice, no income, huge bills coming in, nowhere to work, and to top it all off you are expecting your second child.

One car in the distance. Mine again. The best are the first ones there and often the last ones to leave. To keep a well running business you must spend a lot of time working ON the business vs. just working IN the business. A race car gets worked on all week so it can race well on the weekend. The DC must be willing to work on their business on the weekends, so it can then run successfully all week!
It is often this extra work that keeps a DC from ever getting into trouble.

The best coaching in the world cannot fix a man or woman who was born or develops a desire to lie, cheat, and scheme.

I can go on with more stories like this. Are you getting the idea? I know you are thinking these people are crazy and that these types of things would never happen to you. I assure you these doctors said the same thing.

It is critical to think ahead before doing <u>anything</u>. Having close chiro friends that you confide in and "check and balance" with is a great idea. You want to make sure <u>every move you make is smart</u>!

The two authorities that can cause you the most trouble are the IRS and your State Board of Chiropractic Examiners. The Board can put you on probation, fine you, suspend your license, and take your license away permanently. Imagine having your license taken away.

The IRS can cost you huge amounts of money as they correct your accounting mistakes. Usually when a person finds out they owe money to the IRS, there is no money around to pay it.

The State Board uses the Attorney General's office to do their investigating. The Department of Commerce can even get involved as billing and receiving money from insurance companies commonly crosses state lines. Billing is often done electronically. Insurance fraud is called wire fraud if money transacted electronically and mail fraud if the postal system was used.

We highly recommend you do everything right. Always ask experts before doing anything you are not certain of. You MUST keep your license and be able to practice and earn. You MUST keep all your taxes perfectly current.

Most landmines chiropractors face are self-inflicted. Rarely does someone throw a landmine in your path. It is almost always an 'error in judgement' on the part of the chiropractor that brings trouble. It is hard to become successful when you keep making mistakes and have bad habits.

Other More Common Landmines:

Running out of money when starting a practice:

- A buildout can end up costing much more then you thought. This leaves you scraping to operate and survive while you build the practice. A debilitating feeling.

  This can also occur because the doctor has never had so much money in their account before. They errantly think it will go farther than it does. This error in discipline is usually very difficult to recover from.

  Having enough money left over after the buildout is critically important. ONLY get what you absolutely need to start. Preserve money. Value every single dollar.

  Get the place open, start helping people with chiropractic care, and begin generating income.

Starting with the wrong layout:

- Once the walls are built, electrical is done, plumbing is in place, and ceilings are installed, it is difficult and expensive to change. I just fixed another two-doctor office. I got them to move to a new space and with my design they grew to 386 visits after just two weeks. Using my new layout they grew 50+ more visits a week!

  They were in their poor layout for 9 years not even aware of what it was costing them until I showed them. 9 years x 50 visits a week x $45 per visit = $1,170,000 in lost revenue, without working one minute more! This is enough to pay off both their student loans and their rent for all 9 years!

  Layout and flow are everything.

Spending more than you make:

- Starting out you make nothing. As collections start to increase so does the doctors idea that they can spend more of it. NOT YET! Be patient and pay down debt.

- We call this: *The headlong rush into Gucci-ism.* The doctor thinks they deserve to have nice stuff <u>right now</u> when in reality they have earned absolutely NOTHNG yet.

  Example: A young woman was in dental school. She and her husband lived lean and were very careful with their money. Upon graduation she opened a practice while he kept on with his work. They remained living in the <u>same cheap apartment</u>! They kept driving the <u>same cars</u>! Some didn't even know she graduated because they were still hanging around the same neighborhood.

  <u>They did not change their lifestyle at all</u>. No new fancy apartment or house, no new BMW leases, nothing! As her practice and income grew, they took ALL the extra money to pay off her $227,000 in student loans.

  It took a little while, but they did it and were completely debt free. Zero, not a penny, no bills other than power, heat, cable, and water. Needless to say, they went on to buy a wonderful home and have everything they want today.

  Don't buy anything until you are established financially. Certainly don't buy anything fancy, it will <u>not</u> impress anyone.

Getting lazy with technique:

- Many doctors graduate and think they know enough to be good in practice. Remember, chiropractic schools teach to the least common denominator. A student who graduates and thinks they are "good" at technique is a doctor who is lying to themselves.

  I have been to 38 technique seminars after graduation and have now given over 1,000,000 adjustments. I feel I'm just starting to get the hang of it.

  It takes thousands of adjustments to get good, not the hundreds you did in school. Go to technique seminars and get better!

Wanting a luxury schedule before earning it:

- Plan on being dedicated Monday thru Friday and Saturday morning. Plan to go in on many weekends to work ON your practice. Have a home office and get work done there too.

  A mistake newer doctors make is they see a doctor who is 27 years in practice working only 16 hours a week. They believe that doctor must know how to become successful so they copy that doctors schedule.

  Truth is, this doctor worked 6 days a week for 17 years, now has $800,000 saved, and no debt other than a house. This doctor has earned and can afford a 16-hour schedule. You can't. (At least not yet, but you will if you hang with us!)

Letting yourself go:

- The stress of Board exams, graduation, and working to get started in practice is real. Not to mention a move to a new city or a new state. All this makes it very easy for a doctor to fall out of shape.

- The more physically fit you are the more people will naturally want to come see you. Plain and simple. If you want to take your fitness motivation and habits to a new level go to *innertalk.com* and get some fitness programming audios.

Failure to hire a consultant:

- The time, energy, and money lost from this poor decision is gigantic. You are in a business that requires knowledge and LOTS of it. You need this know-how in your head <u>right now</u>. Your success depends on how much you know.

- The best, hire the best, to become the best themselves.

- The best in any field have coaches. The better they become the <u>more important</u> coaching becomes. Look at sports. The better an athlete becomes, the more important their coaching is. We are exactly the same. In fact, you could easily look at chiropractic as a sport.

- I am 100% confident that if every single DC on earth was a **WINNERSEDGE** member the total volume of patients served on earth would double and the net worth of the <u>entire chiropractic profession</u> would double in a few short years.

<u>Hiring a consultant, only to keep doing things your way:</u>

- This happens all the time.

- There is nothing worse than a doctor having a proven system right in front of them yet they chronically underproduce because they want to do things "their way."

- Winning is not hard. It has already been figured out how to be successful as a chiropractor. There is already a beautiful path to the top of the mountain. There is no need to waste one day trying to invent a new path. Especially with over $200K in student loans. Your care, your art, and your style as a doctor is unique, but the attitude and systems that must be in place to be successful are the same for everyone.

- I tell people all the time: *Your art as a chiropractor is your thing. My job is to make sure you have a super successful art shop!*

I offer you a list of many more landmines. I either see these all the time or have seen them before. There is not enough room to give details and stories on all of them but believe me I have them. Call if you want me to explain any of these potential landmines to you.

- Marrying someone while still in school. Possibly when your esteem was lower, or before you were self-actualized.

188

- A female DC who graduates and right away wants time off to start a family despite owing $244,000 in student loans.

- Not hiring an accountant until it's time to do your tax return.

- Not having an attorney read every lease.

- Failing to have business insurance in place only to have a water leak fry your $35,000 X-ray machine.

- Forgetting to have a Work Comp policy in place. Your CA gets hurt and needs $3800 worth of care that you now get to pay for.

- You like shiny new things and buy every new practice gadget you see thinking it will make you more successful.

- Becoming an unlearner. Acting like your brain is full and that you know enough, leaving your brain-shackled and unable to grow.

- Forgetting to be a growing doctor by keeping up and excited about new ways to help people. Most DCs never learn a new technique after school is out. The pro is always getting better.

- Living 45 minutes away from your office in another town. It's hard to grow when your "life" isn't even close to your practice. In one year you will spend 375 hours driving to work. I will spend only 125. After 5 years you will have spent 78 days in a car. After 20 years you will have spent/lost a year of your life in a car.

- It is worth repeating: Poor location, wrong layout, and bad lease deals are all avoidable problems.

- Choosing a weak, common, or bubble gum clinic name.

- Bad or unprofessional clinic logo and branding.

- Failure to update yourself in ALL online directories. You must Google your name and make sure everything online has your correct name, address, and information. I see doctors who are in Indiana, but when you Google their name, there's an entry that says they are still in Ohio, and another one saying they are in Illinois. *Where are you?*

- Dressing like a "poor student doctor." This is the kiss of death. *Image is ALL* is no joke. John Molloy's great books: *New Dress for Success for Men* and *New Dress for Success for Women* are priceless! Who taught you how to dress anyway?

- Thinking you are burned-out when actually you are bored. Usually caused by being lazy and not working hard enough on your practice and your personal development.

- Failure to understand you are out to build something. What are you building? You build a business card, you build a website, you build a flyer, you build an office, you build a patient base, you build a bank balance, you build a reputation, you build a referral base, you build credibility, you build a great CA team. You build build build!

  If you like building things, you will do well in practice. I love building things. I am building this book right now! Then I will build a plan to get it to all the chiro schools, then I will build a plan to handle the million questions I will have from all the new DCs who want information, then I will build events that will teach them how to be a super success. Build build build!

- Failing to look at every patient as a project. You must LOVE projects and building things!

- Failing to keep a sharp life. Some people build a mess don't they? They build a messy home, a crummy relationship, lousy health, and no bank balance. They build nothing.

  What are you going to build?

Get in the mindset of BUILDING things. You build great dogs through training, you build a cool car from rust, you build a house from an idea, you build a relationship, you build muscle, you build endurance, you build knowledge, you build wisdom, you build experience, you build a practice, you build a great life! Are you grasping how amazing it is what I am teaching you so you can BUILD an incredible future!

- Hanging around the wrong people. I don't have any friends who are not winners. Your relationships, fitness level, practice, and income will be affected by who you hang around. It is okay to not hang around certain people. Winners hang with winners.

- Staying in the wrong relationship too long. Never be too afraid or too weak to end it. KNOW you will attract better for yourself.

- Loaning money to family members. This usually never gets paid back thus ruining many family events for years. *Don't do this.*

- Buying a house before student loans are paid. This requires no explanation but my *Money* book has them if you want to see why.

- Deferring or forbearing loans when you should bite the bullet and start paying them.

- Thinking that having kids will fix a bad relationship.

- Not training CAs well. They should be at most seminars with you if you want them to be awesome.

- Showing up late. Real winners are never late for anything. It is called being a responsible professional.

- Not making your bed every morning. Nothing more basic and essential than this. *How you do anything is how you do everything!*

- Getting too involved in outside activities because "you want to." Being in 3 softball leagues that cause you to miss work when you have NO net worth = foolish.

- Generally, trying to be, do, and have anything you have NOT earned yet. Get this book: *Stop Acting Rich* by Stanley.

- Leasing a car: This is just a way to have a car you really can't afford. Truth is: <u>If you cannot write a check for the car – you really can't afford it.</u> Using this truth, what kind of car could you truly afford right now?

  Until you have NO student loans or any other unsecured debt, learn our auto buying procedure. There is a time a doctor might lease a car but it is way down the road. I have never leased a car.

- Getting scared and making bad decisions.

  Example: A DC finds out his wife is pregnant. He freaks out, gets cheap, adopts a sickening poverty mindset, and thinks he needs to start "cutting costs." So, he quits the $1000 per month consulting group that made his practice successful, only then to see his collections drop by over $5,000 a month.

- Hiring an associate because you think they will help you cover your overhead. You soon realize an associate COSTS a lot in time, energy, and money. They do <u>not</u> make you money. If an associate were to collect $200,000 you will still not break even. If a doctor can collect over $200K on their own, it is unlikely they would be in your office as an associate. Call me for anything associate related.

- You have a spouse work in the office and let your 2 and 5-year-old kids come in and hang out behind the front desk a few afternoons a week. A sure problem as no patient wants to walk in to what feels like your living room. Would a dentist do this? Would any medical office do this? Why do chiropractors think this is okay? The pro keeps home at home and office at office. Yes, spouses working together can be fantastic and kids coming in to get adjusted is also fantastic – just never let it interfere with delivering a patient centered experience.

- Missing seminars. I am amazed at how my $750,000+ doctors seem to be at everything we do, yet the $150,000 DCs are not there. How can you explain this? Be a winner by training like a WINNER. Never miss anything. Once your net worth is over $500,000 you are allowed to miss maybe a couple events a year.

- Thinking that once you are profitable in practice you don't need coaching any longer. Do your patients not need chiropractic care any longer once you have them out of pain? Once you are in great condition do you get to quit working out?

Why ever would you alter the success formula you have created? There is no taking a critical piece out and thinking all your numbers will stay the same.

Fact is: The more successful you become the more important coaching is as you have a lot more going on that requires expert guidance. Trust me on this. Quit coaching = Quit growing.

- Being afraid to meet people. Being scared to walk into businesses and introduce yourself. This is due to ego, low esteem, or who knows what. We all have moments where we want to remain in our comfort zones, but we MUST be able to flip a switch and walk right up to anyone and start talking to them. If you can do this you will have a big practice.

- Billing the wrong diagnosis and procedure codes because you didn't learn how to do it correctly like you were supposed to.

- Inability to tell people the truth and lay out care plans that are correct for each patient. Either because you don't know what the plan should be or because you are too afraid to tell people the truth. I have a few videos on how to solve this very problem.

- Inability to think and plan ahead more than a few days. The pro can think ahead and make plans for projects that will takes years or even decades to complete. Like saving to become a millionaire.

- Ignoring the natural and unwavering laws that govern life.

Speaking of natural laws, there are many that must be understood. In fact, just knowing these and working to honor them will make you an unstoppable chiropractic force.

When success is not occurring in anyone's life, look to see which natural laws of success the person is trying to violate. <u>You can never violate them</u>, they are LAWS. Water always boils at 212 degrees. It will never boil at 112 because you are in a hurry to cook some noodles.

The Law of Cause and Effect says that: *For everything you want, there is a price that must be paid.*

> Most people seem to forget this law. If a doctor calls asking why they are not getting many new patients to come in the answer is simple: *You are not doing enough to get them.*

> Trouble today is, people mistake a little bit of work for a LOT of work. Very few today know what HARD WORK really is. I will show you. A few 4:30 am to 10pm days with a 5-minute lunch break will fix this.

The Law of Vibration says that: *Everything is naturally attracted to that which is at the same vibratory rate. Birds of a feather flock together, so to speak. Misery loves company is lower manifestation of this.*

> *Power vs. Force* by Hawkins illustrates this clearly. Google image this and you will see what I mean. Winners hang with winners!

The Law of Attraction says that: *You are a 'living magnet' and that you inevitably attract the people and circumstances into your life that harmonize with your dominant thoughts, especially those thoughts that you emotionalize strongly.*

The **Law of Gender says that:** *Everything has a gestation period and amount of time required to come into existence. A baby takes 9 months. A crop of corn takes around 3 months.*

Because <u>you</u> want something now means nothing. It takes what it takes IF you do everything right.

No matter what a patient wants, the time it takes to heal is what it is. Ligaments, tendons, muscles, bones, nerve or skin tissue cells take the time they take to regenerate. As chiropractors, we seek to affect the speed and quality of this process.

The **Law of Organization says that:** *Every level of success requires its corresponding level of organization.*

If you are disorganized at 100 visits a week there is no chance of you reaching 200 visits a week. Unless you have been in the Military, you probably have no idea what high level organization <u>really</u> looks like. It must be learned.

The **Law of Substitution says that:** *Your mind can only hold one thought at a time, positive or negative. You can substitute a positive thought for a negative thought whenever you choose.*

The **Law of Habit says that:** *Any thought or action you repeat over and over again will eventually become a new habit.*

Every doctor's treatment time becoming a habit is a classic example. If you have developed the habit of a 2-minute time you can get to 300 people a week. If you have a habit of 5 minutes you will never get past 150 patients a week.

Draw 100 new patients a month and it won't matter if you are unable to see them because your systems and treatment time are too slow. Your treatment time controls your volume, which controls your collections, income, and ultimately your life.

The **Law of Emotion says that:** *A stronger emotion will dominate and override a weaker emotion and whichever emotion you choose to concentrate on grows and becomes stronger.*

The **Law of Expectation says that:** *Whatever you expect with confidence, becomes your self-fulfilling prophecy.*

Expect patients to get better. Expect new ones. Expect great CAs. We get what we unconsciously <u>expect</u>.

The Law of Correspondence says that: *Your outer world corresponds to your inner world. Your life comes from the thoughts which create it.*

The Law of Sowing and Reaping says that: *You have to put in before you get out. You have to give before you receive.*

The Law of Belief says that: *Whatever you believe with feeling becomes your reality.*

The Law of Indirect Effort says that: *You achieve things with people more indirectly than directly.*

A man named Brian wants more friends. Instead of trying to "get people to like him," he should concentrate on *being a great friend* to more people.

With personal relationships you can never change anyone directly. The best you can do is change YOURSELF. Then and only then will others change how they see and treat you. Work hard and become successful, I promise people will look at you differently.

The Law of Compensation says that: *You get out what you put in and the more you put in, the more you get out.*

You will get paid <u>precisely</u> based on these three things:

1. How much demand there is for what you do.

2. How good you are at it.

3. How difficult it is to replace you.

If you are making a lot of money this will be true. If you are not making much it will also be true. It is a law.

The Law of Reversibility says that: *You can develop within yourself the values, beliefs, and qualities you most admire by acting as if you already have them.*

This is why we adjust invisible people and tell everyone we are "seeing 100!" You may only be adjusting 50 patients a day, but in your mind you are seeing 100! *I'm seeing 100 a day!*

The Law of Probabilities says that: *There is a probability for everything that happens.*

The Law of Emulation says that: *You can become like those you emulate, within your natural ability and limitations to do so.*

> This is why we love to visit busier offices then "emulate" that doctor. People are emulating all the time, thing is, they don't know who. The right consultant can be a good person to emulate.

The Law of the Master Mind says that: Not mastermind but Master Mind. *This law states that when a group of like-minded people come together in harmony for a common purpose the group will create a "Master Mind;" giving the group and each of the individuals in the group MUCH greater power compared to operating alone.*

> WINNER**EDGE** is a Master Mind. Every person in the group draws on the incredible power of the ENTIRE group. This makes you much more powerful and much more successful than you could ever be on your own. It is an amazing phenomenon.
>
> Not all doctors can qualify to get in WINNER**EDGE**. We cannot allow anyone in who is out of harmony with winning. Only men and women who can add power to the group are allowed to join.
>
> Most groups will take anyone. We want the doctors who seek <u>to be the best chiropractor who ever lived in their area</u>. We want the men and women who seek to build the chiropractic power life.

The Law of the Habit of Saving: *This law states that as a person develops the habit of saving money, then and only then will they be trusted to handle and hold on to larger amounts of money.*

> This is why our money flow architecture is critical. If the money flow and money laws are being violated, all the new patients and collections in the world won't make any difference.

There are over 100 more natural laws that govern life and success. See them below. Learn more by reading: *The 100 Absolutely Unbreakable Laws of Business* by Brian Tracy.

The Law of Cause and Effect	The Law of Belief
The Law of Expectations	The Law of Conservation

The Law of Control

The Law of Responsibility

The Law of Service

The Law of Overcompensation

The Law of Forced Efficiency

The Law of Creativity

The Law of Persistence

The Law of Customer Satisfaction

The Law of Quality

The Law of Innovation

The Law of the Market

The Law of Differentiation

The Law of Concentration

The Law of Integrity

The Law of Realism

The Law of Ambition

The Law of Empathy

The Law of Independence

The Law of Superb Execution

The Law of Abundance

The Law of Capital

Parkinson's Law

The Law of Investing

The Law of Accumulation

The Law of Accelerating Acceleration

The Law of Determination

The Law of Futurity

The Law of Unlimited Possibilities

The Law of Timing

The Law of Anticipation

The Law of Problems

The Law of Security

The Law of Trust

The Law of Friendship

The Law of Perspective

The Law of Perverse Motivation

The Law of Unlimited Possibilities

The Law of Authority

The Law of Greater Power

The Law of Reciprocity

The Law of Accident

The Law of Direction

The Law of Applied Effort

The Law of Preparation

The Law of Decision

The Law of Flexibility

The Law of Purpose

The Law of the Customer

The Law of Obsolescence

The Law of Critical Success

The Law of Specialization

The Law of Segmentation

The Law of Excellence

The Law of Courage

The Law of Power

The Law of Optimism

The Law of Resilience

The Law of Emotional Maturity

The Law of Foresight

The Law of Exchange

The Law of Time Perspective

The Law of Three

The Law of Compound Interest

The Law of Magnetism

The Law of Sales

The Universal Law of Negotiating

The Law of Win-Win or No Deal

The Law of Four

The Law of Terms

The Law of Need

The Law of Persuasion

The Law of Risk

The Law of Relationships

The Law of Positioning

The Law of Advance Planning

The Law of Looks

The Law of Terms

The Law of Reversal

The Law of Desire

The Walk Away Law

197

It could be said that success is simply your ability to utilize and not violate the natural laws that govern things and people.

There is nothing special required to become successful as a chiropractor. A successful woman <u>will</u> become a successful chiropractor. A successful man <u>will</u> become a successful chiropractor.

You have a mission as a chiropractor. You <u>also</u> have a mission as a <u>person</u> and that is to **become the most high-quality and fully successful human being you can become.** Do this and your practice will follow!

We simply call this "personal development." You will grow to the level of your personal development. Another law!

All these laws can be overwhelming. I now want to teach you something very simple that I have never heard taught anywhere. I personally feel it is common sense gained from years of thousands of interactions with thousands of people in thousands of situations.

THE LAW OF SUCCESS IN SIXTEEN LESSONS COMPLETE

TEACHING, FOR THE FIRST TIME IN THE HISTORY OF THE WORLD, THE TRUE PHILOSOPHY UPON WHICH ALL PERSONAL SUCCESS IS BUILT.

What a statement! But he is right. This book by Napoleon Hill does have the secrets. This is the book *Think and Grow Rich* came from.

<u>Only Four Things Ever Hold A Chiropractor Back:</u>

Now these last four landmines may offend some people. The truth often does. (Being easily offended is actually another crippling landmine.)

In every situation where success is lacking it is because the chiropractor is either: <u>Lazy, weak, cheap, or foolish.</u>

la-zy *adj.* 1. unwilling to work or use energy
2. lack of effort or activity

weak *adj.* 1. lack of enthusiasm, not convincing
2. exerting only a small force
3. lacking the power of character to hold a decision

cheap *adj.* 1. miserly, stingy
2. unable to give what is required to change

fool-ish *adj.* 1. stupid, having or showing a lack of intelligence
2. lacking common sense

Look anywhere in your life where you may be lacking or struggling and one or more of these will be the real issue.

Every story earlier where the doctor got into trouble was because the doctor was foolish, or lazy and foolish, or cheap and foolish. You might even say lazy, weak, and cheap are all forms of being foolish.

NEVER be lazy, weak, cheap, or foolish. The ONLY way to do this is to become aware of yourself and be able to "right the ship" if you are off track. My job in coaching is to keep doctors from being lazy, weak, cheap, or foolish and to correct them when they are.

Smart people learn from making mistakes. The super success learns from other people's mistakes and then never makes them.

Now let's get our mind back on the positive. We always want to think in terms of what we want and where we want our life to go.

ex-cited *adj.* 1. very enthusiastic and eager
2. showing a heightened state of energy

strong *adj.* 1. power to do demanding tasks
2. ability to withstand pressure

gi-ving *adj.* 1. ready to exchange for value
2. to present voluntarily

smart *adj.* 1. having or showing bright witted intelligence
2. attractive, neat, fresh, stylish

You Will Have Many "Firsts" In Practice:

Many will be positive. Some will appear negative, but if you study them you will find that every negative has a positive lesson for you.

You will have your FIRST:

New patient

Medicare patient

Personal injury patient

Newborn patient

Athletic patient

Very large patient

Very old patient

Smelly patient

Loud patient

Patient who prepays

Patient who auto pays

PI check arrive

Medicare payment

Family under care

Re-sign

Person who wants a refund

Positive review online

Negative review online

Surplus of money

Money deficit in practice

Closing due to weather

Power outage

Records request

Deposition

Attorney interrogate you

Referral to an MD

Referral from an MD

Patient you know pass away

Record collection day

Weirdo that calls your office

Employee to hire

Firing of an employee

Patient faint

Employee that quits

Employee that steals

Local DC that dislikes you

First debt paid off

First $1000 saved

First Board complaint

First nice car

First nice house

First major vacation

Equipment breakdown

Day too sick to work

First Holidays as a DC

Goals reached

Phone lines not work

Family event that affects you

Time you owe more tax

Realization taxes are a lot

Record new patient day

Record collection year

And __many__ more. Things are going to happen. Your ability to be cool regardless of whether things are good or bad will serve you well. We like to say: *It just IS. Something is not good or bad, it just IS.*

Respect who got us here:

We are able to practice today because some very smart and powerful people were dedicated. I talk in chiropractic colleges and rarely see their names or pictures, let alone an ounce of appreciation for them. It is so arrogant and disrespectful.

Today many worship at the thought of whoever invented their cell phone, yet thousands of chiropractors have not one word of thanks for those who invented their <u>profession</u>: The great DD and BJ Palmer.

Just imagine if you created an entirely new principle and method then opened a school to teach it. You <u>created an entirely new profession,</u> only to have countless people reap the benefits without ever thinking to thank you.

In some cases, as a chiropractor enjoys the success that chiropractic brought them, they criticize you, and say your ideas are old and don't matter anymore.

Not me. I deeply appreciate the founders of this incredible profession. I thank the many men and women who made everything I enjoy today possible. I could never repay them!

On my website in a section called FREE VIDEOS. I have a great Chiropractic History Lesson that you will find fascinating.

Early Palmer School graduates. Notice the young BJ Palmer's hand on his dad's shoulder. The guy on the bottom right is Thomas Storey. He invented the split headpiece we all use today. At the top right is Solon Langworthy who many credit for our term "subluxation."

The typical chiropractic career is 41 years. How old will you be after 41 years in practice? What year will it be after 41 years in practice?

Since you have come this far, you might as well commit to making the rest of your chiropractic life as successful as possible. We only have one lifetime. There is not enough time to become awesome at many things. Decide today to become an incredible chiropractor. Decide today that you are going to run an incredible practice. Chiropractic at its worst is still better than having a "job."

I see chiropractors who are struggling. Hard to believe when they are in a profession where they can get paid $40 every two minutes when everyone else they know makes less than $40 per hour. I tell these doctors to fall back in love with chiropractic. Many never loved chiropractic in the first place. I tell these doctors: *You better fall in love with chiropractic!* You can't be the best at anything you don't truly love.

I love chiropractic. I love what it is, what it has done for me, what I have seen it do for thousands of people, and what it will do for thousands more.

People ask me all the time: *Tory, what keeps you motivated?* Or they will say: *Tory, what drives you?*

My answer is: *What do you mean?* As if to say: *Is there any other way to feel about chiropractic?*

I am <u>inspired</u>. Those who are <u>inspired</u> don't need outside motivation from anyone or anything.

An inspired chiropractor who has self-discipline is a force to reckon with!

Our BOOTCAMPS may be the only events in our profession today that teach the finer details on how to be a capable and persuasive speaker.

The feedback and experience you can get when practicing in front of myself and many fellow DCs is priceless.

Learning how to speak well to individuals and groups of all sizes in an incredible skill.

Goodwill - The established reputation of a business as a qualifiable asset.

PVA - Better called retention. The average number of visits a patient comes in to see you over time. Total Visits / Total NPs = PVA

Case Average - Average total amount you collect from each patient over time. $1500 is a baseline in chiropractic. Collections / NPs = Case avg.

SPP - Savings Per Patient, a term I invented. Of the amount collected from each patient in a year, how much of it did you save? If you had 300 new patients in a year with a case average of $1500 and you saved a total of $25,000 that year, you have an SPP of $25,000 / 300 = $83. So, of the $1500 you collected from each patient you were able to save $83 of it. An SPP over 5% is incredibly good.

CPV - Collection Per Visit. Average amount collected per visit. Anything over $50 is excellent. Collections / Visits = CPV

Chiropractic - B.J. Palmer's definition of chiropractic reads: "Chiropractic is a philosophy, science, and art of things natural; a system of adjusting the segments of the spinal column by hand only for the correction of the cause of dis-ease."

Want to know what chiropractic is really all about? It is all about TONE. In fact, life is all about TONE. This concept is so smart and amazing it would take many hours to study.

the 5th dorsal; throw to the right.
   Toe Nails. Diseases of.—Adjust 5th lumbar.
   Tone.—Normal tension of nerves, muscles or an organ. The basic principle of Chiropractic.
   Tonsilitis.—See quinsy.
   Toothache. Impingement on the 5th cervical nerve may

Subluxation - State of less energy flowing in the body. Sub = less than. Lux = light, life, or energy. Ation = state of.

Health - Optimal state of physical, mental, and social well-being, not just the absence of disease or infirmity.

Dis-Ease - State of lack of ease in all or part of the body. Commonly caused by subluxation or insults to the body. Lack of TONE in the body.

Disease - Definite pathological process having characteristic signs and symptoms.

Mission - Vocation, calling, or specific task which a person is charged. Our mission is to help as many people as possible with natural chiropractic care. You also have an overriding mission as a human being.

Honor - Keen sense of ethical conduct. Regard with respect. Feeling of responsibility to do things right.

Certainty - Knowing-ness that what you are thinking, saying, and doing is right.

Power - Your ability to make your life the way you want it. Power can also be your ability as a chiropractor to get people better via your care and influence. *A powerful chiropractor.*

ICD -10 - International Classification of Disease. List of diagnosis codes. This is a clinical area that you have to assess for each patient. Every state and insurance company may like different codes. In chiropractic there are only a handful of codes that we use most of the time.

We adjust spines, so our diagnosis code is usually spinal. Since we bill according to spinal region, our diagnosis codes must match. If we bill a 3-4 region adjustment, we better have 3-4 areas with a diagnosis code.

Incidentally, an MD might diagnose "ear infection" H66.90 in a child. A chiropractor would never use this diagnosis code. A chiropractor would use M99.01 - Segmental dysfunction cervical.

Since you are wondering, here are commonly used codes:

M99.0X Segmental Dysfunction Cervical, Thoracic, or Lumbar

M50.30 M51.34 M41.36 DJD Cervical, Thoracic, or Lumbar

M53.0 Cervicocranial Syndrome (Pain into head)

M53.1 Cervicobrachial Syndrome (Pain into upper extremity)

M54.17 Lumbosacral Radiculopathy (Pain into lower extremity)

644.209 Tension Headaches

643.1XX Migraine Headaches

CPT - Current Procedural Terminology. Codes for the services we do. Each has an associated fee. You have to use clinical judgment in the application of all procedures and codes. Most common ones are:

- 99203 Exam   99203-25 Exam with adjustment the same day
- 99213 Re-Exam   99213-25 Re-Exam with adjustment the same day
- X-Ray codes
- 98940 1-2 area adjustment 98941 3-4 area adjustment
- A few therapy codes

Accident - Something a small child does in their pants. They have "an accident."

Crash - When a car or other vehicle of any kind hits or is hit by anything. A car crashes into a pole, a car, a median, a truck, an embankment.

Collision - When two vehicles or moving objects strike against each other. In personal injury work we do not use the word "accident." We more correctly use the words crash or collision.

Casual Observer - A detached, unemotional, professional manner. In reporting information regarding a patient's care we are simply a casual observer of the facts. We communicate accordingly. We are not the patient's lawyer or have any personal agenda. Based on the information available, we are casual observers and calmly render an opinion as such.

Deposition - Event where you are asked questions regarding a patient or incident. A deposition can occur at your office, an attorney's office or other location. They are recorded or videotaped. You get paid for this.

Arbitration - Meeting of involved parties to resolve a dispute. In chiropractic an arbitration may occur to determine if an insurance company should pay your bill for an injured patient. Commonly the patient, their attorney, the insurance company attorney, and the arbitrator are present. It is a faster and easier way to resolve disputes than court.

PIP - Personal Injury Protection. The part of an insurance policy that may or may not pay your chiropractic bills. States and policies have different limits. In a motorcycle crash there may be no PIP for the driver. There may be $2500 or $20,000 in PIP per person per crash. You must know exactly what your state laws are regarding how injury cases work.

Med Pay - Medical Payments. Basically the same as PIP. The part of a policy that pays for medical payments to the injured parties. It is smart to call your own auto insurance agent and have them explain to you exactly how your own auto policy works.

> **Example:** A girl owns a car and has insurance on it. One evening she drives her boyfriend's car to get pizza. He does not have any insurance at the time. The roads are slippery and she slides into a pole while going around a corner. Her friend in the passenger seat is injured and so is she. Both of these girls come to your office for treatment. Who pays the drivers bill? Who pays for the passenger's bill? Where do you send the bills for each girl?

> **Example:** A guy on a motorcycle stops at the light. He notices the car behind him is not stopping so he jumps off the bike just as it is smashed from the rear. He tumbles into a ditch and is hurt pretty bad. He comes to see you. Where do you send your bill?

> Whose Med Pay pays for who? This must be figured out. Each state will be different. Ask a local PI attorney the above questions.

No Fault - Also known as PIP. Designed to cover medical bills if you or your passengers are injured in a car crash. It means that your own insurance covers you regardless of who is at fault. This confuses many patients as they think whoever caused the crash should pay. Only 16 states have No Fault insurance. Injured patients have a lot of questions. You need to understand and be able to explain it very well to all of them.

Initial Care - The first series of visits recommended by the doctor. Knowing what to recommend is critical for each case based on the facts and findings of the case. Most chiropractors don't recommend enough care. I recommend a 90-day initial care plan as a starting point for adults.

Supportive Care - A patient whose condition deteriorates without care is in need of supportive care. Care to hold a person's improvement. *Doctor, if the patient reached maximum medical improvement, why did you continue to see the patient for 43 more visits?*

Answer: *Well, the patient's condition deteriorates without treatment so they require supportive care.*

Wellness Care - Happy and healthy way to term ongoing care to keep a healthy person healthy. Much different than supportive care. Those receiving supportive care wished they were good enough to enjoy wellness care.

Maintenance Care - More boring name for wellness care. Ongoing care at regular intervals, usually no more than once a week.

Everybody can enjoy ongoing chiropractic care.

MMI - Maximum Medical Improvement. Point at which the patient is as good as they are going to get. Often they will be labeled this by the medical world only to come see you and get much better. That is our goal! Sadly however, some patients will never be the same again after an injury.

Image - What people see when they look at you or <u>anything</u> associated with you. Website, business card, office, car, clothes, hair, shoes, micro-expressions, mannerisms, posture, hygiene, fingernails, EVERYTHING! A doctor with a good image will out pull a much more skilled doctor with a sloppy image. Just the way it is.

There is no faster way to get a doctor to grow than to overhaul their frumpy, outdated image with better hygiene and ALL new clothes. The way most doctors dress is a joke. Don't be one of them. I have an entire video series and training on how to dress properly as a chiropractor. I have another on how to read body language. You must be good at reading body language. You must also be great at <u>projecting the right body language</u>.

5 in 15 - A standard I invented where if you have a new patient, a report, a re-exam, a re-sign and a regular office visit <u>all standing at the front desk ready to go</u>. You should be able to see all of them beautifully in 15 minutes. Think about this. How could you do that? What layout is required? What skill level is required?

This is what the busiest, most respected, most loved, most referral generating, highest PVA, and most famous for results chiropractors in the world can do.

Pain - What a patient feels subjectively. The problem gives pain. The pain is never the problem itself. It is just a <u>sign</u> that there is one. *Doctor, it's better today!* Response: *No Jerry, IT is the same, the pain is just less.*

Problem - The thing in a patient that needs to be fixed. The entity that requires a solution. It gets confusing because we say we want to get to the cause of the problem. A fall playing soccer may have caused the subluxation that brings the pain. The patient thinks the pain is the problem, but you will teach them that the pain is just the <u>sign of the problem</u>, which is subluxation.

Subjective - What the patient says. Pain is subjective. Pushing on a vertebra and having it hurt is called tenderness and is more objective.

Objective - What you find. Commonly spasm, fixation, and/or tenderness in the cervical, thoracic, and lumbar region. Remember these. You will forever be asked what your objective findings are. Spasm, fixation, and tenderness are your go-to, but of course it is based on any exam findings.

Assessment - Commonly the diagnosis codes.

What matters?

I was at a Gonstead seminar a few years ago in a class with Dr. Alex Cox. He and his brother Doug bought the Gonstead Clinic over 40 years ago. Dr. Cox represents one of the most experienced and respected chiropractors living today.

As he leaned on the back of a cervical chair he said: *You want to know what it all boils down to?*

The packed room went silent as he said:
Just be good to the person in front of you.
Maybe the best practice advice I ever heard!

Plan - What care you recommend, when, and how often.

Unsecured Debt - Debt that is not directly connected to something tangible. Student loans, a loan from a family member, or credit cards. This is the ugliest of debt that must be dealt with using the WINNERSEDGE *Rapid Fire Debt Elimination Plan.*

Secured Debt - Debt connected to an "asset," like a car loan, home loan, boat loan. (Asset as defined by the bank, our definition of asset is different.)

Asset - Something that puts money in your pocket. Like a bond or a rental property that is generating profit each month. Your practice is an asset if it makes money. If not, it is a liability and you need to call me immediately.

Liability - Something that takes money out of your pocket. Notice your car or house are liabilities and NOT assets.

Honor - High respect, to fulfill an obligation, to hold in high esteem.

Services - Dollar amount value of what you did for the patient using retail fees, sometimes called total charges.

Collections - Total amount deposited in the clinic checking account from all sources for the practice. Also called gross receipts or revenue.

Overhead - Cost to run the business not including doctor pay.

Gross Profit - Collections – Overhead = Gross profit.

Net Profit - Gross profit – Taxes = Net profit. You get paid from this.

Office Manager - A CA who knows how to do everything well and can run the office completely. Any other CAs are just extra hands for the office manager. In some offices, however, the Office Manager refers to a long time CA who has become lazy, off mission, and needs to be replaced.

Clinic Director - You as the doctor are technically the clinic director but I like this as the title for my main CA. It makes them feel good and looks great on a business card or resume. This is a person who can run an office well. Billing, phone skills, patient interactions, and all skill sets are excellent. Maybe 10 CAs in 100 are at this level.

Associate Doctor - An employee who legally can see patients. There are very specific criteria for adding an associate. Most DCs have no idea what they are and cost themselves hundreds of thousands. It is never smart to base a huge financial decision on an illusion of what you "want" vs. what is reality. I see doctors all the time who invent new and amazing ways to take home less money: Adding an associate is often one of them.

Phantom Payments - All the additional costs associated with owning anything. Expenses that you can never predict but are always there. This is why if a house payment is $1500 per month you can count on at least another $500 a month in phantom payments to live there. There is NO avoiding this. Another law, the Law of Phantom Payments!

It is commonly taught that if a house costs $200,000 and you live there 30 years, you will spend another $200,000 on the house during that time, not including any interest on the loan.

Referral Statements - List of great phrases for the doctor and CAs to say to patients to spark referrals. Like: *Remember John, we are here to help your family and friends too!* We have a great list of these for our clients plus the procedure for using them to create more referrals.

Recall List - List of all the patients who are not in the appointment book that you would like to see again. We have a procedure for this.

Treatment Time - How long the doctor takes per patient in seconds, not minutes. There is a HUGE difference between 3:12 and 3:57.

I will now describe something nobody really understands even though they are bound by it every day. It is so simple that it confuses people. It is so truthful yet people argue with it. Nothing changes the fact that it is true. We will call it the Law of Treatment Time.

The chiropractor with a typical 10 shift schedule will have around 900 available minutes per week for direct patient time. The rest of the time is for notes, walking around, talking to team, phone calls, going to the rest room, reviewing X-rays, making care plans, and everything else.

If you want to see 200 patients per week you will need to average 4.5 minutes per person. 900 minutes / 200 visits = 4.5 min. avg.

If you want to see 300 a week you need to average 3 minutes per person. 900 / 300 = 3 min. avg. This includes new patients and reports!

There is no fighting this. There is no: *But I want to spend 10 minutes with each patient and see 300 a week.* This is what we refer to as being delusional. A doctor may not know they are delusional until I show them with facts and hard numbers.

Always remember that time is your biggest constraint. Becoming very good at delivering quality in short periods of time is a highly valuable skill for any chiropractor. We call it *compressing quality.*

Graduation from chiropractic college is just the first phase of your chiropractic education. All the required business, practice and success training that follows is the second phase.

To truly reach your potential in practice and as a person takes organized training. Just like an Olympic athlete has organized training, we must also if we want to be a champion in our field.

Seminars, bootcamps, private coaching, audio material, video material, interacting with those much more successful, having those at your same level to grow with, and having newer DCs to share and teach are all necessary for a doctor to become their best. I estimate only 10% of chiropractors seek to be the best. Will you be one of them?

Serious Questions:

- *How many patients do you really want to see in a day?* _____
- *How many patients do you really want to see in a week?* _____
- *How many new patients will you average per month?* _____
- *How much do you want to collect every month?* _____
- *How much do you want to collect every year?* _____
- *How many seminars do you plan to go to every year?* _____
- *Where are you going to learn all the procedures and systems?*
- *Where do you plan to learn the business skills required to practice?*
- *Where are you going to learn how to save and pay debt the fastest?*
- *Who are you going to emulate? Are they really worth emulating?*

To be thoroughly successful in practice today takes an incredible amount of know-how. There is no time to "figure it out on your own."

The sample with random names below shows what it's all about. See the result of high-level coaching, training, listening, and applying. A doctor will come to me not doing as well as they know they could.

They can engage the WINNERSEDGE system and now see a typical day. This is 164 visits in <u>one day</u>. Only one chiropractor in 100 will ever get good enough to do this with patients happy, paying, and referring.

Those with small thinking sometimes say: *You can't give good care unless you spend more time with people.* This is hilarious and simply not true. My reply is: *Those who know what they're doing can do it fast.*

If you get really good at delivering what your community wants, a lot of them will <u>want</u> to come see you. The doctor has <u>no choice</u> but to become efficient enough to serve everyone that wants to come in.

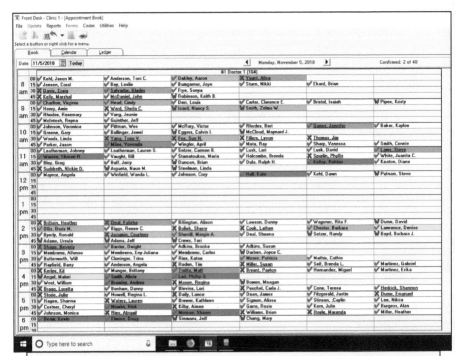

Exactly as taught. 6 columns wide with scheduling done laterally. It is always a goal to fill an entire hour solid. Notice from 5-6pm every spot is full. In this sample we need to go to 5-minute increments instead of 15 and add a 7th column. This will reduce the pressure and actually cause more growth. The correct layout is required to control the space, the correct appointment book is required to manage time and accurately match what is possible in real time. Most DCs have their appointment book all wrong.

There is nothing whatsoever within the four walls of a chiropractic office that I am not considered one of the world's foremost experts.

After reading this book be sure to read very carefully our: *Money Chiropractic and You - Thoughts and solutions to the most difficult practice questions.*

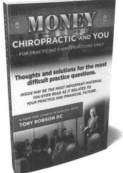

You will love what you learn. This book can be worth literally millions to you! We give this away to any chiropractor who asks.

How to choose a practice consultant:

The best coaches:

- ❑ Still work inside a cranking practice and still see patients.
- ❑ Do or have owned commercial real estate.
- ❑ Are or have seen the volume you want to see.
- ❑ Are or have collected what you want to collect.
- ❑ They are a legit millionaire.
- ❑ They are physically conditioned.
- ❑ You can visit their office <u>and</u> their home.
- ❑ They have a facility designed for training chiropractors.
- ❑ You actually get "the guru" for personal coaching calls and not some assistant coach or worse yet, you are part of some group calls with no one-on-one clear leader expert.
- ❑ Have created hundreds of instant videos for you on all elements of how to do everything.
- ❑ Has put the effort in to publish many audio sets and books on chiropractic success <u>for you</u>.

There are many DCs who have done well and want to give advice. Like with athletes, very few of them are any good as coaches. The completeness of the program, videos, audios, events and direct coaching will reveal a lot about how powerful the program is in its ability to actually <u>cause</u> growth and change.

Only great and unselfish teachers become great coaches.

High energy seminars are essential. We draw on the massive power of the group, then go back to do more than we ever could on our own. Our seminars are held on Saturdays from 9 until 4. We then have a social hour after that everybody loves!

See and have fun with other super successful doctors and teams. Imagine what you can learn when you are surrounded by winners! *People grow where people grow because people grow where people grow.* You grow here!

We have Workshops in my own office. We do a few a year on the Friday evening before our Saturday seminars! This is where everything from technique, to procedures, to speaking skills, to care plans, can all be trained in a real office!

While the CAs are in a breakout room the doctors can discuss and handle all team management issues. Doctors require doctor only training time just like the CAs need CA training time. Knowledge brings great power. We deliver the knowledge.

I have personally spent over $220,000 on myself for coaching, seminars, and success materials of all kinds. Those who want to be the best spend what it takes and connect with the best coach to get them there.

How to handle difficult people and difficult cases are discussed in our "Pit Classes." If you have any practice issue we can cover it here. Being able to get 20 experienced opinions instantly when you have a concern is priceless.

The smartest and most relevant training material is what makes a great event. You must leave knowing more than when you arrived, and be inspired to go back with a new level of power and confidence.

The most successful doctors in the group are invited to become what we call WINNERS**EDGE** **GUARDIANS**. At this level, additional training exclusively with myself and other high performers is on the agenda.

The best never wind down. We are always winding up! Set a goal right now to become a WINNERS**EDGE** **GUARDIAN**.

The WINNERSEDGE DC **BOOTCAMPS** are the most physically and mentally demanding events in chiropractic today. Our incredible **BOOTCAMPS** are one of our many secret weapons designed to hammer you into the person you are truly capable of!

Physical training is mental training but not the other way around. We use genius level methods that utilize workouts to burn in critical goals, attitudes, and scripting. Practically everyone breaks a practice record within a few weeks of the Bootcamp.

Considering what people <u>see</u> makes up 97% of communication, you should learn how to dress. Who taught you how to dress anyway? There is a <u>science to this</u>. People buy what they see. We will get you looking better than you ever have before!

There's only one way to get better and that is by drilling over and over. Your success hangs on how you <u>look</u>, then knowing what to <u>say</u>, when to say it, and how to say it well. Only then will people let you <u>do</u> anything.

216

We can have the smartest and most successful guest speakers *Zoom* in live from anywhere in the world. Here we have Dr. Demartini *Zoomed* in from Tokyo. By many accounts, he is the most successful chiropractor in the world today.

Our first self-made, new era billionaire *Zooming* in with us. Prepare to have your mind blown. Hang with the highest level people and you too will become high level. Nobody has what we have here!

Many things that we do at the **BOOTCAMPS** are CLASSIFIED, but simply know you will have more fun, learn more, grow more, and be more electrified to conquer the world than you ever have before in your life. The stronger you are mentally the more successful you are.

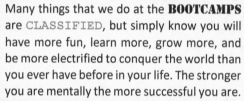

The most successful doctors are usually operating quietly. Take Kevin Wilmot here for example. 150 visits per 4-hour shift, three-time Ironman, husband and father of 3. You will not find higher quality men and women anywhere.

We get nowhere without a great team! Our CA training is incredible. Breakout trainings at every seminar, audio sets, videos, plus they can attend many workshops and... we even have a CA **BOOTCAMP** exclusively for them! No wonder our offices are so successful!

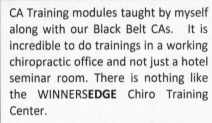

CA Training modules taught by myself along with our Black Belt CAs. It is incredible to do trainings in a working chiropractic office and not just a hotel seminar room. There is nothing like the WINNERS**EDGE** Chiro Training Center.

The CAs get serious image training as well. Many offices suffer because their CAs don't dress properly.

Drilling the key responses to all patient questions, phone skills, making payment arrangements, generating referrals, dedication and *FIRE for chiropractic* are all on the agenda.

CAs work hard too! A sit up circle at the end of a killer workout followed by a nice catered dinner poolside at my house! Hard training + a great time!

A chiropractic office does not require much to be operational and successful. Adding therapy and wanting employees is normally what causes a doctor to require more space.

I will deliver this in bullet form. This topic would take a book all on its own so I can only give the outline here. Call me if you want coaching on how to do this and win.

What type of doctor is this style of practice for:

- One who likes to work alone.
- One who is more of a minimalist.
- One with practically no money to get started.
- One who can and wants to do it all themselves.
- One who wants tremendous freedom in practice.
- One looking for a way to get started and expand later.
- One with strong philosophy who likes a pure chiropractic model.

If you want to own a simple chiropractic office and you have very little money, here is how to do it:

1. Find a 10' x 12' or larger room to rent inside an existing business. It could be a gym, gymnastics center, multi-story office building, law office, accounting office, insurance office, bank, or anything in your area. Walk in to all of them and ask if they have a room.

2. Engineer a deal where your rent is free or close to free. In exchange you will care for all the employees of that business or something else of value to the business owner.

    Make a brief lease for 12 months with an option to continue for another 12 months. Lay out what your small % of any utilities may be. Perfect fairness is the goal here. Of course, an attorney reviews any leases before signing.

3. Renting inside another chiropractic office is a last resort as the host doctor will want you to pay half of all the bills, the very thing

you want to avoid. However, this is a possible option we can discuss if the opportunity presents itself.

4. All smart location criteria still apply. Parking, easy access, and at least a few chairs somewhere in an existing lobby will be important.

5. Clean the room and floors and paint every wall. Make the room feel as clean and new as possible.

6. Equip the room with chiropractic posters, books on a shelf, and a model spine.

7. Get a desk and a 2-drawer file cabinet. These can be found at a used office supply store for a sweet deal.

8. Get the least expensive adjusting table that will work. If it costs over $1000 you can lease and make payments to preserve capital.

9. Load the file cabinet with hanging file folders and copies of all required forms. Storage of anything will be done at home.

10. Use Facebook as your website for free.

11. Use an existing computer or laptop. Get it cleaned and tuned up if necessary. Do not buy a computer if you can avoid it. Get a simple black and white combination fax, scanner, printer.

12. Your cell phone, or a second cell phone added to your plan will be your clinic phone. Make an appropriate voicemail greeting.

13. Get business cards made and printed at *vistaprint.com*. Remember every dollar counts so keep it nice but low cost.

14. Use *Office Ally* online for billing. Try not to buy or get hooked into any large monthly payment for chiropractic software.

15. All legal elements to opening a chiropractic business still apply.

16. Check to see if you need business insurance on your room. You may be covered by the host business since you are in their space. Offer to pay your % of the business policy.

17. Buy your malpractice policy and make sure all your information is current with the State Board and Secretary of State.

18. Put all WINNERSEDGE scripting and money flow in place.

19. Important: We recommend adding an A or B to the address. Instead of 1247 Maple Street, call yours 1247A Maple Street. Google, the postal service, and others appreciate this.

20. Know exactly what you are selling as far as your Consult, Exam, Report and Office Visits are concerned. Remember our quote from Beckwith: *The first step in marketing a service is the service itself.*

    What exact service are you selling? Professionalism is the key here. Lazy, sloppy, cheap looking chiropractic is NEVER acceptable. Be thorough, complete, and excellent.

21. Connect with a local chiropractic office to take any needed X-rays. Work out an agreed upon fee structure for this.

22. Visit the local MRI Center and get referral pads.

23. Get referral pads from a local orthopedic MD or neurologist.

24. ALL normal practice start-up elements apply. We are simply doing it all in one room with little or no rent and no staff.

25. Consider an answering service to cover the phones when you are unable.

26. Use the Square App for credit card payments. Use *Fortis* for automated payments.

27. Use any online calendar as your appointment book. Consider *Genbook*.

28. You can either do a full paper SOAP note as seen in our Forms set. *Office Ally* and *Patient Ally* allow you to do notes in the computer. This is normally slower. We only use computer notes if they are required to get paid. If not, a good paper note like we have will work well.

29. Be able to handle all 5 types of patients: Cash, Medicare, Work Injury, Personal Injury, and regular Insurance.

30. Make sure you have a smart email address. No college or goofy email addresses ever. Have one that looks more "doctorly."

31. Once you're ready, it is time to market and promote like crazy. Use our *90 Day Practice Explosion.*

32. Every morning, leave a new voice greeting and let people know what your day entails. *Good morning this is Dr. Johnson and it is Thursday March 15ᵗʰ. I will be in the office today from 9 until 12:30 then back in from 3 until 6. If you are an existing patient feel free to come in then. If you are new and would like to visit with me, also feel free to come in during those hours and I will work you right in to my schedule. Otherwise, please leave a message. Thanks, and have a great day!*

33. Make sure your schedule is clear on your business cards, any door signs, and online.

34. Train every patient where to wait and how your system works at this location.

35. Your primary codes will be 99202-25 and 99203-25 for exams and 98940 and 98941 for adjustments. Price them properly.

36. All the above can be done for $4000 - $7000. The goal for fixed overhead every month is under $2000.

37. Treatment time and doctor discipline is what makes this work. A doctor who is easily controlled by patients will get stuck in the room, making other people wait and become unhappy.

38. I have doctors right now seeing 50 patients a day in one room.

Example 1:   40 patients per week

<u>$40 collected per visit</u>

$1600 per week x 4 weeks = $6400 per month

Example 2:   70 patients per week

<u>$40 collected per visit</u>

$2800 per week x 4 weeks = $11,200 per month

Example 3:   120 patients per week (30-40 a day)

<u>$40 collected per visit</u>

$4800 per week x 4 weeks = $19,200 per month

Example 4:   200 patients per week (50 a day)

<u>$40 collected per visit</u>

$8000 per week x 4 weeks = $32,000 per month

Considering the low fixed monthly overhead, this allows a doctor to be profitable very quickly. The money saved on rent and staff is enormous.

I have designed the one room, two room, and three-room offices of the future. The plans were shown earlier in this book. How to do it and make the plan work is what takes expertise.

Chiropractic offices have been started a certain way in the past. This does <u>not</u> mean that is what is best for you in the future.

Our goal is the nicest office with the lowest overhead possible. This is a MAJOR KEY to business success. If a doctor is always stressed out over making their monthly overhead it only means two things:

1. They need to work harder and produce more. (This is the primary problem in nearly all cases.)

2. They have an overhead issue.

I even see doctors who need to <u>increase</u> their overhead in order to collect more. They are unable to see it until I show them.

Regardless of what style of practice you want, the right coaching will get you there!

Success Essentials List

AUDIO SUCCESS ESSENTIALS

- ❑ All WINNERSEDGE True Chiro Success Audio Sets - *Robson*
- ❑ Chiropractic Philosophy - *Reggie Gold DC*
- ❑ The Magic of Believing - *Claude Bristol*
- ❑ The Science of Getting Rich - *Wallace Wattles*
- ❑ The Strangest Secret - *Earl Nightingale*
- ❑ How to Become A Millionaire - *J. Earl Shoaff*

VIDEOS

- ❑ The Chiropractic Debate - *Reggie Gold DC*
- ❑ Joe Straus Lay Lecture - *13 min of Joe Strauss* (Incredible!)
- ❑ How to Have Your Best Year Ever - *Jim Rohn*
- ❑ All Jack Lalanne Videos (He was a DC that never practiced.)
- ❑ All Dan Kennedy Videos
- ❑ You Were Born Rich - *Bob Proctor*
- ❑ All WINNERSEDGE DC Training Videos - *Robson*

BOOKS

- ❑ Are You the Doctor, Doctor? – *Barge* (Read all Barge books)
- ❑ Money Chiropractic and You - *Robson*
- ❑ Chiropractic Philosophy - *Strauss*
- ❑ Evolution or Revolution - *BJ Palmer*
- ❑ Secrets of the Million Dollar Practitioner - *Fernandez*
- ❑ The Science of Getting Rich - *Wallace Wattles*
- ❑ The Strangest Secret - *Earl Nightingale*
- ❑ The Greatest Salesman in The World - *Og Mandino*
- ❑ The Richest Man in Babylon - *George Clason*
- ❑ The Laws of Success in 16 Lessons - *Napoleon Hill*
- ❑ As a Man Thinketh - *James Allen*
- ❑ How to Solve All Your Money Problems Forever - *Victor Boc*
- ❑ Selling The Invisible - *Harry Beckwith*
- ❑ Think and Grow Rich - *Napoleon Hill*
- ❑ The Definitive Book of Body Language - *A & B Pease*
- ❑ Rich Dad, Poor Dad - *Robert Kiyosaki*
- ❑ The Bible New American Standard (*Read Book of Proverbs first.*)

True Chiro Success products

Turn your car, office, and home into a chiro success training center. Listening to smart audios, watching success videos, and attending live events are the best ways to grow. School is never out for the pro!

Here Is the Reality We are In

A smaller percentage of people go to a chiropractor today than did 10 years ago. <u>Chiropractic is not growing.</u>

The current market demand for chiropractic is definitely there but it is thin. It's nothing like other health care services such as medical care, dentistry, physical therapy or massage.

The competition is **extreme**. DCs are over-saturated in many areas. There are 52 chiropractors in my city alone. Even with our CREATE mindset, a town can only support so many DCs.

The local market rate for a chiropractic visit of $35 to $60 is the same now as it was 20 years ago, despite the cost of living going up dramatically. **To give you an idea:** an office visit was $38 when I started in practice and a new Corvette was $42,000. A chiropractic visit is <u>still around $38 per visit</u>, but a new Corvette is $70,000.

The typical chiropractor's student loans have nearly doubled. I owed $130,000 and now they average $244,000. This means a DC now has to collect over $1,000,000 just to pay their student loans!

Health insurance to cover chiropractic is getting worse with high deductibles, lower reimbursements, and lower maximum benefits. Very few people have any insurance, but most of them <u>think they do</u>.

There have been decades of disagreement among chiropractors, chiropractic colleges, and chiropractic associations on matters regarding the definition of chiropractic and how it should be practiced.

Inconsistent messages about chiropractic are being told to the public. Chiropractors resort to professionally embarrassing promotional schemes like: $39 per month for unlimited care or $39 for 15 minutes.

It doesn't help that some chiropractors use treatments that make no sense in the public's eye. More chiropractors than ever are going to jail for fraud, fee splitting, and other things. In the last year 21 chiropractors in my area have been in the paper and on the news for breaking the law.

This has scared away thousands of potential patients and discouraged other doctors from routinely referring patients to chiropractors. I look at chiropractors and ask: Where's the chiropractic?